P9-CCX-990

NOV 2 7 2014

bespotted

Also by Linda Gray Sexton

•

HALF IN LOVE
Surviving the Legacy of Suicide

SEARCHING FOR MERCY STREET
My Journey Back to My Mother, Anne Sexton

BETWEEN TWO WORLDS
Young Women in Crisis

ANNE SEXTON
A Self-Portrait in Letters

FICTION

•

RITUALS

MIRROR IMAGES

POINTS OF LIGHT

PRIVATE ACTS

bespotted

my family's love affair

with

THIRTY-EIGHT
DALMATIANS

· A MEMOIR ·

LINDA GRAY SEXTON

DISCARDED
BRADFORD WG
PUBLIC LIBRARY

COUNTERPOINT · BERKELEY, CALIFORNIA

Bradford WG Public Library
425 Holland St. W.
Bradford, ON L3Z 0J2

Copyright © 2014 Linda Gray Sexton

All rights reserved under International and Pan-American Copyright
Conventions. No part of this book may be used or reproduced
in any manner whatsoever without written permission from the
publisher, except in the case of brief quotations embodied in
critical articles and reviews.

Library of Congress Cataloging-in-Publication Data
Sexton, Linda Gray, 1953-
Bespotted : my family's love affair with thirty-eight Dalmatians / Linda
Gray Sexton.
ISBN 978-1-61902-345-1
1. Dalmatian dog. 2. Human-animal relationships. 3. Sexton, Linda
Gray, 1953- I. Title.
SF429.D3S49 2014
636.72—dc23
2014014414

Cover design by Natayla Balnova
Interior design by E.J. Strongin, Newirth & Associates, Inc.

COUNTERPOINT
2560 Ninth Street, Suite 318
Berkeley, CA 94710
www.counterpointpress.com

Printed in the United States of America
Distributed by Publishers Group West

10 9 8 7 6 5 4 3 2 1

For Alfred Sexton
August 5, 1928 – May 11, 2012
my champion

For Myrna Robinson
November 20, 1949 – December 21, 2011
my ally

For Gulliver
June 14, 1997 – May 28, 2010
dog of my heart

contents

Prologue   1

PART I
Mother's Miracles
10

PART II
Our Very Own
52

PART III
Literati Dalmatians
88

PART IV
Dog of My Heart
104

PART V
New Beginnings
150

PART VI
Keeping the Vigil
166

PART VII

Afterward

182

PART VIII

We Wait

202

PART IX

The Puppy Pen

220

PART X

Going Home

246

PART XI

A Different Sort of Dog

260

Acknowledgments

275

"If there are no dogs in heaven, when I die, I want to go where they go."

—WILL ROGERS

prologue

THE STORY OF MY family's life with the tribe of thirty-eight Dalmatians that romped through our years together is the story of a crazy kind of love affair. How was it possible to love, so relentlessly, this single, particular breed, one often described with words like *neurotic, nervous, hyper, skitzy, overexcitable, snappish,* and *downright nasty?* The Sextons, however, believed staunchly that those who held such mean-spirited opinions were wrong. Instead, we used words like *loving, companionable, lively, mischievous, exuberant, happy,* and *smart.* We had always rooted for the underdog, perhaps because we were underdogs ourselves, crippled by the shadow of my mother's continuing mental illness. As an artist who spent her hours creating a radical new kind of poetry, my mother always counseled us to look below the surface, to see the possibilities of every day around us. And these dogs fit into that category of unrealized potential quite neatly.

When I was a child, Dalmatians were the breed we adored, unequivocally; Dalmatians were the breed we always picked when one beloved dog passed on, and we had to choose another as quickly as possible, as was the custom of the times. No prolonged or cathartic grieving for us. When one member of the family was gone, we filled the void, right away—preferably with a soft, cuddly pup who would undoubtedly pee from one end of the house to the other or chew up prized objects like slippers, glasses, baseboards, and rugs.

In a home where my parents were both inconstant and inconsistent because of my mother's illness and my father's anger, the dogs became symbols of absolute love, of fortitude. If they could survive such difficulties, so could we.

My love for the intensely colored dogs did not wane as I created a new family of my own. I took it with me, the way one would carry forward a love of climbing steep mountain peaks or swimming in deep lakes. None of these dogs were perfect. All had their idiosyncrasies. But each and every one dropped into our lives much more happiness and joy than they did anger and frustration. As I brought my first dog home to my own children, it never even occurred to me to consider any other breed. Dalmatians were in my blood.

• • •

It is 2013, and fifty years have passed since my parents brought home our first Dalmatian. Many things have changed in that time. For one thing, every month, the mailbox is crammed with stacks of catalogs, even though it isn't yet Halloween. I am sixty now, but I still haven't figured out how to unsubscribe from the thick, glossy books. I keep only the ones specifically designed to tempt the dog owner—*In the Company of Dogs, FetchDog, PetEdge, L.L.Bean*'s for Dogs, *Frontgate Pet*—and even the one from RC Steele, which is directed toward breeders or those in the "fancy," as dog showing is sometimes called.

I pore over heated dog beds with coordinating kidney-shaped pillows, dog ramps, dog hammocks. Cooler wraps, puppy-weaning pans, hair ribbons for poodle pompadours, electric shears with interchangeable blades, and toenail grinders with diamond-tipped wheels. Agility tunnels and weave poles for smart dogs, interactive puzzle toys for the couch potato. Grooming tables for the animals who will be shown in the ring, heavy-duty hair dryers for thick-coated breeds, snoods to keep longhaired dogs' ears out of their chow bowls.

These encyclopedic, slick "magazines" are as alluring and rich with goods as the stalls of a Middle Eastern bazaar. I can't wait to get my hands on each and every one. Just to look and laugh. Just to look—and sometimes buy.

I am a dog lover, a dog breeder, and I try to be a dog person as well. As a dog lover, I enjoy *nearly* all dogs (no one wants a rabid Cujo)—despite matted coats and various peccadilloes. I often hang out with my dogs instead of my friends, eat peanut butter and jelly while my dogs dine gourmet, and think my dog is a good kisser. My dogs have almost as many toys as did my kids when they were little.

I want to pat most canines coming down the sidewalk without having been properly introduced, and I frequently cuddle up with other people's dogs even though I am getting covered in long, clingy hair. I don't mind getting the two-paw nice-to-meet-you jump—even though I draw the line at muddy feet—or having my ears washed with a long pink tongue. I can frequently be caught cooing "baby talk" to total dog strangers, and I have friends whose dogs have their own pages on Facebook, with pictures of their human families as well as their best canine friends.

I am also a breeder, devoted to preserving the specific characteristics and health of our particular breed—while raising carefully timed litters of the spotted variety. Responsible breeders attend seminars on everything from puppy rearing to correct structure to evaluating temperament, and we happily consume most books on the subject; often we have traced our dogs' family trees back further than our own, searching for far more than good looks. We do what "puppy mills" and "backyard breeders" do not: check for certifiable results from independent canine medical organizations that attest to a particular dog's "clean bill of health." Eyes, ears, thyroid, hips, elbows, and even DNA are evaluated. Only after a thorough screening for congenital defects is complete does a good breeder choose to pair a sire and dam.

We usually belong to several organizations—some local and some national—that educate, and we promote the ethical guidelines that ensure the welfare of all dogs, and of our breed in particular. Recently, I have begun to seek out rescue work, willing to drive a long distance to transport a lucky dog—whether abandoned puppy or old-timer—to his "forever" home. I am also grateful that I have the ability to make financial donations. Last, but not least, I always accept my own puppies back when placements just don't work out.

Though Dalmatian breeders sell their puppies, they usually do so at a loss, as the asking price for a pup rarely equals the costs involved in raising a sound litter: health investigations of both parents; expensive stud fees; round-trip airfare for transporting the prospective mother back and forth to her mate; vet bills for both regular prenatal checkups and any kind of complication that may develop, such as premature labor or a Cesarean section; dewclaw removal for prevention against tears further down the line; two sets of shots; having the litter both hearing tested and microchipped; and all the daily expenses such as bedding, cotton balls, and puppy chow. I am often asked why a sane person would take on so much expense for so little return, and the answer is an easy one. For the love of it.

Finally, I am a "dog person," someone who tries to understand why dogs do what they do. A dog person does more than just love. She tries to discipline and reward in a way her dog can truly understand; she tries to lead just the way a parent does; and she tries to appreciate both the young pup's exuberance and the adult dog's wisdom—even when it is frustrating to do so. Perhaps most important, a dog person tries to recognize that if she can be humble enough—like a dog—even a table scrap can be a full and tasty meal.

I was nine when my family got our first Dal. We had two cats, and my sister and I watched three litters of kittens be born in the darkness under my parents' bed. But kitties weren't sufficient—a dog it had to be. The reason it was a Dalmatian was definitely complicated: certainly it was for the joyful demeanor of the breed, their innate sense of humor, their steadfast devotion to their human counterparts, and just their striking good looks—characteristics that run contrary to the popular misconceptions that all Dals are deaf, or make only great fire truck mascots, or are to be prized solely for their lush and extraordinary coats, courtesy of Cruella de Vil.

But even more importantly, my parents adopted our very first Dalmatian because my mother's best friend had one, and they were prone to imitating one another down to the smallest of details. If it was good enough for her family, it was good enough for ours. We romped with these dogs at Maxine and Vic Kumin's summer farm and cuddled them in our laps. As with so many other people, this first introduction to a specific breed of dog spun outward throughout our lives. My family went on to own a series of Dalmatians, and when my sister got her first dog, it was also one of the spotted variety. It was inevitable that I, too, would follow their lead. At this point in my seventh decade, I can't even imagine leaving this life without a Dalmatian's head on my lap as I pass on to wherever I am going.

. . .

At my twenty-fifth college reunion, my friends and former roommates—and I, of course—pulled snapshots of our children from our wallets, displaying them in their sports uniforms, holding up their trophies. However, at my thirty-fifth reunion, it was photos of our dogs on cell phones that made the rounds after dessert, accompanied by the same muted sounds of appreciation and delight—and the inevitable competitiveness. "Your golden chases a Frisbee?" one friend repeated, a self-satisfied smile on her face. "My Otto loves to charge his water dummy—but then, Labs are just natural-born bird dogs."

I myself succumbed and showed off my elderly male Dal, who could manage no trick in particular, except to look distinguished. I admitted to being a Dal breeder, aware that some of the public looked down on fanciers of a particular full-blooded breed—and the American Kennel Club as well—preferring to rescue mixed dogs from shelters. While I had respect for their choice, there appeared to be a stigma against purebreds, and so I grew quiet about the subject.

On the flight back home to California, I thought about both those dinners ten years apart and wondered: *Kids then, dogs now. Why?* For the first time in decades, I finally had the opportunity, freedom, and wherewithal to travel, stay out late, or even just sleep in on a relaxing weekend. Gulliver, the family Dal the kids had grown up with, was just becoming a senior, well settled and easy to care for, and still not at the stage where he would have special needs. And yet this was when, like so many of my peers, I chose to tie myself down once again to the schedule and needs of a new puppy.

I got an eight-week-old to keep my older one company, even though it meant more sleepless nights, gritty-eyed mornings for the 6:00 AM kibble run, and leaving parties earlier than others to go home and walk the animals. I used dog-training manuals as I had once used Dr. Spock. Again I had puddles on the carpets and tiny teeth marks in my sofa legs. The baseboards were gnawed on till they ceased to have corners. Getting a companion for Gulliver was the excuse I dreamed up for myself just when the reign of dog hair drifts and stinky cow hooves was nearly at an end.

With embarrassment, I confided to a close friend that perhaps the real reason I had brought another Dal into my house was partially because I was really scratching another itch altogether. I had been cooing at babies in strollers, admiring small-size booties and knitted caps for quite a while. I wondered, would this relentless urge ever leave me? Was it permanent? As my children hit their thirties and I climb wearily out of the pit of menopause, I discover I have a touch of what my friends and I now call "Grandma Lust."

In a *New York Magazine* article, writer John Homans talks about the increase in oxytocin levels that we undergo while gazing into our dogs' eyes, which mimics the increase in the same hormones in our systems when we bond with our human infants. Dog owners recover at a faster rate from heart problems than do non–pet owners. Pair bonding such as this stimulates social affiliation and trust, and in this way, dogs become our role models. Eighty-four percent of dog owners consider their dog a child.

So I got a puppy instead of doing a late-life adoption. Bringing this different kind of joyful youngster into our home,

I traded housebreaking for toilet training, obedience classes for detention, and a pet sitter for a babysitter—wildly unlike any of the things my family had done with our Dalmatians when I was a child. At the six-month marker, I signed us up for "puppy kindergarten," a modern invention that socialized my new offspring just as I had once entered my sons in a similar institution that had taught them to cope with their peers. And just as I had felt nervous about my sons' first days at school— would they behave, would they have separation anxiety—I now worried about similar things for my pup. Later on, being lousy at a retrieve would be the equivalent of being lousy at figuring the angles of isometric triangles in math.

· · ·

Maybe I have dogs now because they tap into that part of my maternal instinct that had only gone into hibernation when my kids took off for their own apartments—that part of my personality that I am often unable to lavish on my friends or my new husband. Dogs have always provided a special kind of love and companionship that I experience only some of the time with humans. They have a strong sense of character and live the way we ought to: dogs neither compare you to your sister nor make judgments in her favor. Dogs never know what is coming and so live purely in the moment, savoring the good, doing their best to endure the bad—and they offer up this miraculous example so that we can learn from it, becoming role models of a sort. Dogs are radically different than the partners who sometimes give up on marriages, or the friends who get angry over real or imagined slights. Dogs never just get up and leave.

It is no surprise, then, that 78.2 million dogs live with owners in the United States today, and that there are more dogs in American households than there are children. The advent of a new dog in my home has always been a way of staying connected to life—a life that can, at times, be lonely or difficult.

Isolated behind the keys of our computers, we live enmeshed in an age dominated by email and social media, both of which purport to keep people better connected—even though there have been times when I have learned over the Internet that my son has a new squeeze. Sometimes I wonder if Facebook and all its spinoffs really demonstrate only how far apart we have actually grown, as we desperately create daily bulletins of meaningless activities for all the world to see: I don't really want to know that the schoolmate I haven't seen in fifteen years had meatloaf for dinner last night, or even that a close friend packed her car for vacation in less than an hour. It is much more satisfying to have some communion with my dog instead.

As columnist Ben Stein says of his relationship with his German shorthaired pointer: "When I want a peak experience, I just lower the shades and get in bed with Julie and my Mozart discs, and I am in heaven." As my husband observes, "When I die, I want to come back as one of Linda's Dals." Or as my stepdaughter puts it more simply: "Dogs rock."

My life has been blessed with ten adult Dalmatians, as well as three litters of eight each and a fourth of six. A total of thirty-eight spotted dogs, when you tally them up in this particular way—without double-counting those who were born into my household and who then stayed on. Each of them shaped my life in one important way or another. I have loved enough of them to know quite a bit about the unusually devoted disposition of the breed. Not enough to be an expert, for as far as Dals go, there are no experts. They are always surprising you—occasionally for the worse, but most often, for the better.

mother's miracles

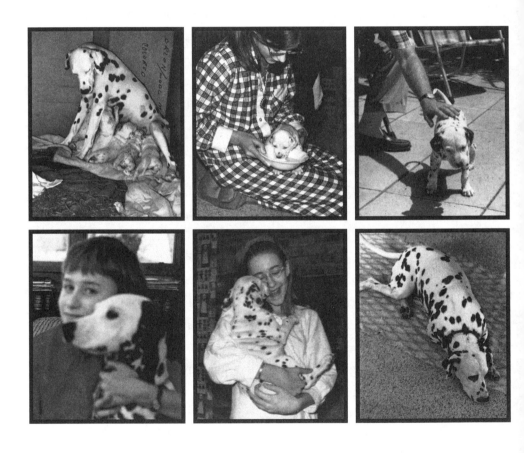

{IN ORDER OF APPEARANCE}

Penny

Eight Puppies

Clover

Angel

Sherlock

Gidget

Daisy

one

NOW, AS I LOOK back over my sixty years, I realize that sometimes it is in the nature of miracles not to occur in a crisis, but in the most mundane of circumstances, blossoming out of everyday existence into something as yet unrecognized. It was five thirty in the morning on that dark winter weekday in 1966, the floor chilly beneath my feet. I was about to turn thirteen. I yanked up my bedroom shades to reveal the snowbanks of our Boston suburb and the streetlights that still shone over the black ice of the road. Neither my parents nor my sister were yet awake. I had gotten up to wash my hair before my father made breakfast and the seven o'clock school bus arrived, and as I dialed the thermostat in the hall up to 68 degrees, a peculiar noise threaded through the silence of the house, with high-pitched intermittent squeaks and squeals. It sounded like the nest of rats that had taken up residence under the barn at camp last summer. I tiptoed down to the first floor, searching, uneasy. The sound grew louder. When I reached the door to the basement stairs, it hit me: in the stillness of this quiet dawn, life was arriving.

I ran to broadcast the news to my parents and my sister, Joy, calling through the hall between the bedrooms in a loud but shaky voice, and then bounded down the stairs three at a time to return to what we had all been anticipating for weeks.

In the wooden pen my father had built, from inside the cave of a large cardboard box that had once held a case of toilet tissue, birth was taking place.

For the last two weeks, our Dalmatian, Penny, had been incarcerated in the basement—amid the old rocking horses, the discarded rolls of rugs, and an old television set without an antenna—heavy-bellied and lethargic, waiting for her time. Every night during the past two weeks, when I gave her a good-night ear scratch before going to bed, she had looked up at me from her chair with what seemed an expression of abandonment in her light brown eyes. Why, she seemed to ask, must she be banished to a damp place where no one lived, filled with shadows and the cat's litter box? I felt a wave of sadness for her then; she had been alone, perhaps not understanding what was happening to her. Every night as I turned out the overhead light, I wondered if the next day would bring us the puppies Joy and I so longed for and allow Penny to return among us to the land of the living.

Inside the big cardboard box, two puppies crawled blindly, bumping up against the sides; their mother didn't take notice of them, or perhaps she simply couldn't. For, as I watched, Penny heaved and panted, heaved and panted, whimpered and then pushed, hard. And at last, a dark slimy bubble the size of a baby's slipper slid out in a whoosh of liquid from the space between her hind legs.

Now she worked with proficiency and tore open the sack with her teeth, working savagely yet delicately, and a slick body tumbled out onto the bed of shavings. Lowering her muzzle close to the puppy's body, she began to chew on the thin spaghetti-like cord still connecting the two of them until it severed. Only then did she return to a pup that still lay without moving and begin to lick it hard, and as she did so, it began to move, just a little at first and then with more vigor. Out came the first mewling sound. And the pup began to turn from dusky blue to rosy pink, still wet and slick. The skin was covered with black spots, but within minutes, as the pup dried off, its wet coat turned snowy white, and the spots were hidden beneath what I now realized was fur.

As soon as she had nudged them closer to herself, she half rose on her front legs as if to gain better purchase and began to strain again; another body emerged slowly, appearing just a bit at first and then slipping back. Finally the bloody bag slithered out. Nausea cramped my gut at the grisly sight, a bath of blood and mucus and the dark mass of afterbirth, that, I realized with horror as I stared down into the pen, she was quickly eating. Was this really how it was meant to be?

My sister and my parents came down the stairs in a wave, filling the room with noise and activity, and I felt less anxious and alone. My father began to search the whelping box for more puppies and discovered two wedged into a corner, crying weakly but insistently as they looked blindly for the warmth of their mother's body.

My mother sat and smoked a cigarette, musing it seemed, perhaps caught up in a quiet awe at the way life was unfolding in our basement, right at her knees. She was a woman fascinated with death, having tried to kill herself innumerable, uncountable times. The puppies' arrival, however, brought a vision of abundant life into her psyche—and thus into our lives—on that day.

Joy jumped around happily, helping my father dry off the new pups carefully, having run back upstairs for towels, and settled them in next to Penny, who was, even as the pups tried to stay near her, pushing out another. Her panting had increased, and she no longer pitched herself forward onto her front legs to deliver another whelp. Exhausted, she had begun to rely on her humans to help out.

. . .

My parents had neglected to spay Penny when we got her as a young dog in the autumn months of 1966, just as they neglected to spay our two cats, both of whom had litters before they were taken to the vet to ensure that it never happened again. And so, shortly thereafter, just as biology dictated, Penny came into heat with her second cycle, probably around her first birthday.

A little behind on the uptake, my parents shut her in the backyard with its six-foot fence, topped with pointed pickets, confident that she could not get out. But Penny clambered right up that expensive fence for an assignation with one of the neighborhood Lotharios, a mutt named Herbie, who belonged to my best friend.

Horrified by the idea of a litter of mongrel pups, my parents rapidly decided to breed her again the next day, intentionally this time, to a friend's Dalmatian boy, hoping that his seed would swim faster than Herbie's and rescue them from the situation. A female dog's "seasons" allow for multiple implantations over the course of several days, so it was not implausible that she could either get pregnant solely from Caesar, or else, from some mixture of the two.

Caesar arrived with Maxine and Vic Kumin in tow. Maxine was my mother's writing cohort, best friend, and big sister. They had both become poets at the same time and had risen to similar levels of prominence in the early sixties (and both eventually went on to win Pulitzer Prizes). It made perfect sense that Maxine would supply the male, one without papers I believe, for Penny, definitely without papers. Both dogs had been sold as pets and undoubtedly the contracts between the new owners and the breeder stipulated that neither Penny nor Caesar be bred—if there had been any contracts to begin with, of course. Neither dog was a candidate for the show ring for a variety of reasons: breeders use only the best exemplars of the breed when deciding which dogs and bitches should be bred, as a way of keeping a Dalmatian looking like a Dalmatian and a Doberman looking like a Doberman. Both the American Kennel Club and the Dalmatian Club of America would certainly have frowned on the sort of union we were about to achieve, ironically now known in the fancy as a "backyard breeding," which ignores both pedigrees, health certifications, and registration papers.

Apparently, Penny was as ripe as a peach. Caesar chased her all around the backyard, and Joy and I—having been banished offstage by my parents—snuck to watch from the living room window, noses pressed against the glass. Penny scrambled up on the picnic table, but Caesar cornered her before she could even jump down again, and in an instant, he nailed her right up there for all to see. He pumped away, tiptoe, his front paws hooked up nearly at her shoulders to restrain her. Then they stood absolutely still, locked together. However, after a few minutes, he made what seemed an unwise decision and began to turn and dismount. In a moment, they stood still joined, their noses pointed in opposite directions, looking like Siamese twins stuck together rump to rump. They just stood there. Then Caesar tried to move again, and they tumbled off the table onto the ground.

Even this did not dislodge him. Joy and I ran through the house, screaming, "They're stuck! They're stuck!"

My father and Vic turned the hose on the dogs, swearing and panicked, dousing them with a stream of cold water. It didn't work. Nor did trying to pull them apart. Nor did standing there and speaking to the soaking-wet, shivering dogs with gentle words. These dogs were not about to relax and let go. Joy whispered to me in shock, "They're going to have to cut his penis off!"

It seems that not even the adults knew that the dogs were doing something natural. Part of the breeding process is a "tie," where the canine penis, trapped inside the female by its complicated anatomy, acts as an effective dam until the sperm has a good chance to swim up the canal. Eventually enough time passed that Caesar deflated and was released.

As Penny had expanded, looking more and more uncomfortable as the all-too-short sixty-three days of gestation raced by, my mother and father repeatedly said they would destroy the puppies when they came if they were Herbie's offspring. Joy and I were horrified and begged them not to do it. But my parents didn't want to be stuck with a litter of pups that could not be registered, thus reducing the possibility of selling them and practically ensuring that they would have to give them away. They didn't need the money, and there were practically no costs involved, as they did not follow through with things like dewclaw removal or hearing testing, and as the breeding itself had cost them nothing but one afternoon's entertainment. But for some unstated yet persistent reason, it seemed crucial that they sell the pups. Thus they enlisted the help of our housekeeper, Mary LaCrosse, getting her to promise to help them drown the pups if they were "mutts."

Joy had nicknamed her "Mary the Cross" during our early childhood because she yelled at Joy constantly for making messes in her bedroom and at me for spilling soup down the front of my school dresses. She had been with my mother's family since my mother was a child, and she was an adored member of the household. My mother loved and depended on her. For many years, Mary lived on a farm with her husband, Fred, and six sheepdogs, and it was fabled that many of the dogs slept in the bed with them. Once, when my father stopped in at the farm on an errand, he found her up to her armpits in the manure pile, filling a wheelbarrow with which to fertilize the garden by hand.

Mary lived a gritty life on her own and often came to work in a stained housedress, her shaggy black hair wild, sometimes smelling of sweat. Or of sheepdog. Despite these traits, which belied the conventional stereotype, Mary LaCrosse somehow knew how to keep things clean and tidy. Our messy household was uncared for by my disinterested mother, and Mary knew how to change sheets, how to "fan" the magazines on the coffee table, how to straighten out my mother's desk without misplacing a single paper, how to train the dogs we would one day own, and, unlike my mother, how to really cook: slow-roasted chicken swimming in butter, egg-salad sandwiches on soft white triangles of bread, and deep-scented lamb hash from leftovers. Perhaps most important of all, she knew how to manage my mother because she'd been doing it for my mother's entire life. My mother listened to her obediently and would even stop writing a poem midstream so that Mary could dust and vacuum her writing room.

Despite an obvious affection for dogs in general, "Me-Me," as we called her, had disposed of several unwanted litters in her time. She agreed to help my parents fix the error they had made by being late in spaying Penny. But when the early morning of the birth arrived, it was Mary's day off.

After watching for a bit with Joy and me in the poorly lit basement, my parents found themselves unable to go and get the pail put aside for the purpose of the planned euthanasia. And shortly it became obvious that it wouldn't be necessary because all the puppies born were Dalmatians.

At the time the puppies arrived in 1966, my mother was in the midst of writing *Live or Die*, her third volume of poetry, the one for which she would eventually win a Pulitzer Prize eight years before her death. Up until that point, and despite the title that revealed her ambivalence, much of the book had been occupied with her death wish, including poems like "Suicide Note" and "The Addict."

After the eight puppies had been settled down and Penny had at last been made comfortable enough to sleep, my mother went upstairs to her typewriter. As the sound of the little cries floated up from the basement to her writing room just at the top of the stairs, she began to create a new poem called "Live." In its final stanza, she credited the birth of the puppies for her own increasing mood to do just that—to live. The puppies had worked like some magical incantation, transforming her into a state of gratitude.

> So I say *Live*
> and turn my shadow three times round
> to feed our puppies as they come
> the eight Dalmatians we didn't drown.
> Despite the warnings: The abort! The destroy!
> Despite the pails of water that waited

to drown them, to pull them down like stones,
they came, each one headfirst,
blowing bubbles the color of cataract-blue
and fumbling for the tiny tits.
Just last week, eight Dalmatians,
¾ of a lb., lined up like cord wood
each
like a
birch tree.
I promise to love more if they come,
because of cruelty
and the stuffed railroad cars for the ovens,
I am not what I expected. Not an Eichmann.
The poison just didn't take.
So I won't hang around in my hospital shift,
Repeating The Black Mass and all of it.
I say *Live, Live,* because of the sun,
the dream, the excitable gift.

The poem would become one of her most famous, the centerpiece of the book that would win her a national reputation. To the family, it symbolized my mother's return to us, how she had at last turned away from the blackness that tortured us all. It was her rejection of suicide, if only for a time. The Dalmatian puppies had cheated death.

• • •

It seems to me now that my mother's reaction to the birth that day was a miracle. Even at the age of thirteen, I was able to recognize that it presaged a new era, however short, of a buoyancy in her frame of mind. Perhaps I recognized it, even at that early age, because she had me read and critique the poem, perhaps because she smiled at the kitchen table over her late-morning coffee and greeted me happily when I returned from school each day.

The birth of the puppies returned my mother to us and re-inforced my already deeply seated love of animals, Dals in particular, and all that accompanied them: from the birthing to the dying. Dogs provided both joy and solace, bringing with them a special connection—even though it was one that must eventually, inevitably, be severed. And because that connection could not last forever, it was even more precious.

two

IN 1953, I CAME home from the hospital of my birth to a small, intimate neighborhood with houses closely set together, their patches of lawn spread out in neat squares in the front yards. There are black-and-white snapshots of my mother posing in the car with the door open, a squinty-faced baby wrapped in a woolen blanket in her arms. My mother had come from a family where an infant nurse in starched white took care of the babies, and her mother had always been a distant figure. She had no real role model for being a hands-on parent. To say she looked overwhelmed and somewhat helpless, as well as pleasingly proud, would be an understatement.

Our house was red brick, with green shutters and a big oak tree out front at which my father was always cursing, as it housed a bevy of gray squirrels that dropped acorns down into the grass, over which he labored like a slave in an attempt to have the most perfect postage stamp of green on the street. Up and down he went with the fertilizer spreader, laying the white powder out in unwaveringly straight lines. He liked to shoot at the squirrels with his deer rifle, and I never forgot the day he actually hit one of the speedy devils, the coiled red guts blossoming out the side of its belly. I accepted it then as "his way," but I was nevertheless repulsed by it. It seemed to me both unnecessary and cruel, even if it was as small an animal as a squirrel.

There, all the dogs roamed the streets. No one kept them in fenced yards, so we got to know them, each and every one: Tippie, the friendly brown-and-white mix who lived across the street, and Max, the black terrier who lived next door and liked to dig up my father's precious lawn, among others. All my friends had dogs. I was envious of the warm comfort this seemed to bring to their lives. I envied them their canine pets and the peaceful—or so it seemed—atmosphere of their homes. They were what my grandmother called "normal." The father went to work. The mother oversaw the children; made breakfast, lunch, and supper; sewed; and made coffee cake for the church bake sales. Nothing was like that at my house: my father worked as a traveling salesman who spent his time eating up the highways from New Hampshire to Virginia, but my mother worked, too, it appeared, from her desk in the dining room, where she hunched over her typewriter keys. It was Nana, my father's mother, who did the sewing, the child raising. My parents fought all the time, and my sister and I huddled together during the angry altercations. I often prayed for a dog, who would have brought comfort.

We had two cats, and though we loved Rosie and Violet—both of whom were strays taken in from out of the cold—they weren't the same as a dog who would run after you, tail flying, keeping pace as you roller-skated down the sidewalks. They weren't the same as a dog who would pad out the door at your heels as you joined the other kids after supper on balmy summer nights, when the ice cream truck rang its bell as it slowly cruised the street, drawing in everyone under sixteen. My friends' dogs sat watchfully, tongues lolling, hoping for a spill, as we ate our Nutty Buddy cones or grape popsicles.

Even Nana had dogs, two Boston terriers who were always getting into fights. We loved Jingo and Bingo, but they weren't ours. Later would come two West Highland white terriers, Piper and Lori, both show-quality animals with extensive pedigrees hung on the walls, but destined to loll about as pampered pets.

My mother's parents raised and showed Old English bulldogs—so perhaps for me, owning and raising beautiful show dogs was preordained. After my grandparents' death, an enormous silver punch bowl, which was engraved with both the names of the kennel club who sponsored the show and the winner, graced the buffet in our dining room, holding the plethora of Christmas cards that came through the mailbox slot in the front door every year, rather than the more traditional eggnog for which it had surely been designed. When my mother died, I inherited this bowl and, initially, used it for the very same thing. Now I display it on the living room bookshelves along with all my other dog trophies: it was the first in a nice long line.

My father, too, wanted a dog, one with whom he could play as he had played with his childhood dogs, a dog big enough to be a "dog" but not as big as a pony. And so, finally, in 1962, my parents gave in to our whining and brought home our first. Clover was a lively Dalmatian, just as warm and affectionate as I had hoped, though she wasn't allowed to sleep on my bed, as I had fantasized. She came from a farm in New Hampshire close to Maxine Kumin, who spent her summers away from her own suburban neighborhood beside ours.

Our town, Newton Lower Falls, had been named for the waterfall that separated it from Newton Upper Falls, and its river divided it from the upper-class town of Wellesley; the Fig Newton cookie was named for the town, which was near the biscuit factory that manufactured it. There was no supermarket, barbershop, or pizza place. Just a liquor store that my grandfather owned for a while and a drugstore where we went for Hershey bars and the chewing gum that came in slim packs of baseball cards, which we girls traded to the boys for pieces of the flat pink bubble gum.

I remember Maxine as a big Dalmatian fan, but in any case, her Caesar was bumptious and fast with a thrown ball. Joy and I loved playing with him. When the breeder who had whelped Caesar had a girl up for sale, my father, a softie underneath all his violence toward the squirrels, listened to our entreaties and bought her for us as a surprise. In this way, Clover joined our band of six, my mother and father, Joy and me, and the cats.

My sister and I loved Clover's moderate number of black-and-white spots and her soft brown eyes that were so welcoming. She had a narrow head that made those eyes particularly luminous. Immediately, I fell in love with the beauty of the Dalmatian breed and did not want any other kind of dog, not even the "neater" ones owned by the families of some of my other friends. Belying the stereotype that all Dals were hyper with nasty temperaments, she was gentle and loving.

Every morning, Clover cuddled up on the worn red chair in my mother's writing room, pleasing her mistress with some friendly company as Anne clacked away furiously on her beige manual typewriter and endlessly revised the poems that were already making her famous. Clover was the first in our family's long affectionate relationship with the breed—a dog with the "soulful" eyes my mother found so irresistible. Sparkling under our praise and love, she was the perfect pet for a home with two growing children and a stay-at-home, lonely mother-poet.

Another of Clover's favorite activities was to sit in the middle of our street, holding her paw up to cars that came to abrupt stops in front of her. The year I turned nine, and sometime close to when she turned two, she also developed a wanderlust that often took her far from home. It seemed my parents were always searching for Clover in my mother's Volkswagen Bug (nicknamed the Blue Jewel) or my father's black Buick Electra (a company car that he hated to use for transporting the dog even to the vet, as her white hairs penetrated the upholstery and clung to whomever had the misfortune to sit in the passenger seat).

"Clo-Ver," they called in loud, singsong voices as they drove slowly through the neighborhood, usually just as dusk was beginning to fall and they at last realized she had been missing since early afternoon.

She loved to roam over the golf course that ran behind our house, just on the other side of the railroad tracks, and my father worried (when he could worry about someone other than my mother) about the dog being hit by a train. This planted a fear in my heart. My parents never took Clover out on a leash because no one walked their dogs in those days, at least not in our neighborhood. Never once did they confine our beauteous wanderer to our nicely sized backyard by building a fence. The denouement of her freedom was not a surprise.

It was a sunny autumn afternoon, probably in 1962, when I was nine years old. It was getting late, and the sun was just lowering itself to a slanted angle in the clear blue sky as we returned from the community play in which I held the starring role. It was an afternoon tinged with the success I'd experienced in a performance that had been applauded for a long time; an afternoon tinged with the smell of leaves burning, in the days before it was politically incorrect to pile them high and wide along the gutter and throw in a match.

Our next-door neighbor, Les, came running into the front yard to say that Clover had been spotted down on the highway that bisected Newton Lower Falls from Auburndale. Route 128 was one of the new interstate superhighways, built just a few years before. It was four lanes in each direction, with cars speeding by in busy, tightly packed lanes. My father and Les went running, but it was already too late.

I imagined her body spinning high into the air and then landing with a sickening, bone-crunching thump. I don't believe my father even brought her home because she was so mangled. The police took her straight to the vet, perhaps, some place from where she could be disposed.

Overwhelmed with grief, my mother picked up Clover's china water bowl and threw it into the sink, where it shattered. We all cried, long and hard. My performance in the play was forgotten. We had lost our first companion animal, the one with whom we cuddled, the one who never failed to prick her ears for a photo opportunity, the one who first showed us what a true Dalmatian smile was, with her lips wrinkled up in a friendly, silly grin that showed her front teeth. Our first animal comfort, full of life in a house where death so often threatened.

My father did not wait long to bring home a replacement, in an era when people didn't allow themselves to fully grieve a dog before seeking another in order to recapture the bliss they had experienced with the first. We called her Angel, but an angel she was not. At four months old, she was still a cute puppy with loving round eyes and floppy ears too big for her head. However, she steadfastly refused to be housebroken, thus contributing to my mother's general sense of chaos and loss of control. In those days, housebreaking was undertaken by using a thick layer of newspapers on the floor until the dog was big enough to go outside. We did not understand that we were teaching them only to poop and piddle inside the house from the very first day. No wonder Angel was such a trial.

Even with Me-Me giving advice, and using a rolled-up magazine to smack her on the bottom, or shoving her nose into her fragrant piles—nothing seemed to work. She kept right on piddling and pooping on the newspapers spread, more and more abundantly, all over the kitchen floor. Needless to say, she wasn't allowed out into the rest of the house, and because of this, we had trouble bonding with her. My mother had long since been brought to tears by what was seen to be Angel's intractability. No more dogs to comfort her, no more warm presence in the red chair of her writing room.

Me-Me, banging a pot with a spoon behind the puppy's head, declared that she must be deaf. Deafness runs in the breed, but only at birth, and becomes evident as soon as a puppy's earflaps open, at three weeks old. At that time, most breeders relegated such pups to the "farm" soon afterward, but somehow Angel's deafness had escaped notice. When my parents took her to the "farm," I imagined this to be some bucolic spot where deaf dogs could run free and not worry about being housebroken, but now I suspect that this was just a euphemism for the end of a vet's fatal needle. Little Angel disappeared out of our lives, and we never had a chance to know her. I can't really remember what she looked like, and there isn't a single picture of her in the family scrapbook.

three

I MET MY THIRD Dalmatian in the summer of 1964, when I was allowed to go off for my first year at sleep-away camp, a place where I learned to be independent. For a while, I had been begging to spend a month at Highlawn Farm, a girls' horseback riding camp near Maxine's summerhouse in New Hampshire. Her daughters had gone there for several years, so it was a place my parents felt safe in sending me. For me it meant freedom from the demands of my mother, whose mental illness increasingly pressed down on the family. At camp I didn't have to take care of her, and I didn't have to worry about her either. And at camp, best of all, there were horses.

Highlawn was in the mountains outside the tiny town of Warner, which was basically just a crossroads with a small IGA grocery store, a post office, and a Laundromat. It was a working farm with cows and chickens raised in order to be slaughtered for winter meat and "outside" dogs that ran in a pack around the pastures with the small herd of sheep and goats and cows. A full vegetable garden had bird nets and staked tomatoes, which were later on the table fresh in summer and in winter from glass jars, whose seals made a pop when you opened them. A baler picked up the hay we mowed in careful rows and compacted it into the squares with which we fed the livestock.

The horses were carefully bred in the paddocks, both mare and stallion supervised by the owners of the farm, introduced to each other at the end of leather leads, then the mare's tail carefully pulled to one side so that the stud could enter her. All of us girls perched on the wooden fence rails like attentive sparrows, fascinated by this primal scene. The animal life around me was a relief from the interior life of the mind and the psyche by which life back in Massachusetts was driven.

Foals had just arrived every year I attended. The breeding of horses was another connection to life, and so horses were now included in the adoration I felt for dogs, in much the same way they are for so many teenage girls, who are not yet ready for romantic love with a boy.

In the aftershock of Clover's death and the banishment of Angel, my heart was empty, ready for a new infusion of dog love, someone to curl at my feet as I did my homework at the kitchen table, someone to playfully hide his head between his paws in a favorite game of hide-and-seek. His name was Sherlock, for no reason I can remember, but he made an indelible impression as I arrived from Newton, homesick for Clover, if not for my mother.

Sherlock was a striking young Dalmatian pup, and he immediately caught my attention. Like the more misbegotten Angel, he was also deaf, and he had been dropped off at Highlawn because of this handicap. Here he could run free and perhaps survive. Like Clover and Angel, Sherlock was lively and loveable. Perhaps loving Sherlock was really just another chance to love Angel.

While the dog pack circled the campers warily—their main contact was not with humans—Sherlock let himself be petted and his ears fondled. He had a large black patch running from his left ear down over his eye, and this gave his face a delightfully lopsided look. I loved his soft black-and-white coat, the way his spots grew from the size of dimes up to the size of rough-shaped quarters, the way some of those spots stood singly and others ran together in slightly crooked lines, and of course, his ears of bold black. Apart from the patch on his face, he could have been a show dog, but I knew nothing about show dogs at that time and so knew only that he looked beautiful to me.

At Highlawn, the ten summer girls were really worker bees for the owners, Liz and Ted and their family, and for the farm from June to August, a span that provided nearly all of the main income for the farm throughout the year. Winters were downtime; everything and everyone at the farm bundled up for the freezing wind and snow, the summer girls long gone home. Sometimes I was allowed to come with Maxine and her daughters to Warner during these quiet months at the farm, and we rode from Highlawn's barn in air so freezing it numbed fingers without gloves instantly, as well as feet clad only in thin leather riding boots. The horses' hooves crunched through the snow, and there was no cantering, but how happy I was for this precious time. And how grateful we all were for Liz's generosity in warming us up over her dinner table.

But those two summer months were not forgotten by a single one of us, and we pined to get back to camp full-time. For $200 a month—a sum our parents gratefully paid—we were allowed to take care of the animals and give riding lessons to those more wealthy, privileged girls who went to camps modeled on Teela-Wooket, those "real" riding camps that catered to richer families, where programs included horses *and* swimming lessons, archery *and* riflery, arts *and* crafts *and* tennis.

But the way we saw it, we were the lucky ones because we had constant physical contact with the animals and a summer-long riding lesson as well. Every morning before the "customers" arrived, we mounted up on the ponies and horses we had fed and curried and hoof picked and tacked. While we disliked mucking out the stalls—boot soles matted with clumps of manure and straw—we took a perverse pleasure in it as well and just hated those interlopers whose names and numbers filled the grimy, ink-smeared lines of the appointment book.

Hot afternoons were spent cleaning tack: our fingernails rimmed with dirt and greasy saddle soap, one thin dime assuaged our thirst with an ice-cold orange soda or root beer pulled up from the old-fashioned red Coke machine that stood in a corner of the grain room. It was only a matter of time before Joy's lobbying to come to camp forced my parents to relent; she followed me to Highlawn after a couple of summers, just shy of when she was old enough.

The riding ring, nothing but a dirt track encircled by a split-rail fence, threw up constant clouds of dust that coated our arms and faces. The haze created, lit by the high summer sun, made it hard to see without shading your eyes with your hand. Sherlock liked to stand with his nose through the fence, watching the horses curve around in their circle on the track, or he ran in and out, threading his way through their legs as their riders awaited their turn. No one took mind of him; he had become a fixture from the day he arrived. He had no fear of the large iron-shod animals, Dalmatians having originally been bred to run in the traces behind horse-drawn carriages and then to guard the passenger's luggage and boxes during overnight stops at the inns along the way, town to town. It was a long time before the breed became associated with riding on fire trucks.

The first month we learned something as simple as posting to the trot, but by the second year, we had progressed to railroad ties laid on the flat, carefully spaced to serve as cavalletti, or a fence crisscrossed at only eighteen inches high. And by the following July, it would be a broad jump at three feet and riding the far-more-difficult sidesaddle. Both Joy and I made steady progress, becoming extremely proficient riders over the course of a few summers.

By my third summer, I got to pick a mount for myself alone, a magical experience that cost $100 extra, money I made babysitting rambunctious kids for twenty-five cents an hour during the school year. Instead of my favorite mare being worn out with the constant riding of others, she was fresh and all mine for the two months I stayed at camp.

For eight weeks, life revolved again around the horses, the chickens who needed to be fed their corn, the goats and sheep who needed their hay spread out in the pasture, the dogs who begged for kibble in their bowls. Day to day, we did it all, and kept the calendar for the incoming customers as well, aiming the feet of little girls into their stirrups, straightening the reins of those our own age, and showing them all how to post up and down in their English saddles by giving them a boost with our hands.

Secretly, we laughed behind our hands at how terrible all the incoming riders were. We took groups of adults out for trail rides, shepherding them through the woods over paths barely discernable to the eye, through the ferns, through the mud and streams, and through branches that sometimes had to be held back from one rider to the next in order to allow the line to pass. We liked this better than teaching in the long afternoons, which were hot and dusty and full of dull stupid girls kicking our beloved animals around the ring. Besides, on a trail ride, you got to ride rather than just stand there, yelling instructions. It was a treat that enriched the day's early morning lesson.

There was a tribe of cats—kittens and mothers alike, led by the males—who served as main mousers for the barn, and were not fed at all, left to forage on their own. The dogs sniffed along hungrily, Sherlock at our heels, all of them waiting to be fed but hoping anyway that some sweet corn and grain would fall when we hefted the buckets and poured them into the horses' feed boxes.

I loved the way Sherlock joyfully sped willy-nilly over the acres of the farm, barking at the cows, pestering the goats by nipping playfully at their heels and making them run round in circles, giving the chickens a scare and stirring them up in a great flap of squawking and dust.

As a latecomer, he didn't really hang out with the pack of other dogs, none of whom I remember, and that made him even more dependent on humans. He followed us girls from activity to activity, interested, it seemed, in everything we did. He had to be restrained from following us into the woods when we took out customers for trail rides, and he wanted to be in— but was banished from—our sleeping area. However, when he was successful at getting past the counselors, he made a warm nest at our feet in our sleeping bags, where we lay on top of our shaky army cots.

On the hot summer evenings, when we were taken to a nearby lake to swim, he was allowed to join us, a special treat, and he was the only dog taken in the metal bed of the pickup truck, where my eight compatriots and I held on to our butts and shrieked with laughter as we swerved and bottomed out on the ruts of country roads. Sherlock swam like a retriever and loved to jump from the muddy bank into the cool water, not hesitating to chase sticks or to swim out in deep water to the raft that belonged to someone we didn't know and who apparently didn't care that a bevy of girls used it as a place from which to dive.

Highlawn had no programs for Red Cross life-saving instruction, or speed racing, or even perfecting a jackknife, just the enjoyment that came from washing the day's thick layer of dust off our burgeoning young bodies in the soft, lukewarm water, which we let dry on our arms and legs as a way of cooling down in the summer night. And then it was time to go home. The smell of sodden dog fur filled the air in the truck, and as we went to bed and threw off our flannel sleeping bags, our hair wet our pillows, silky and cold against the napes of our necks.

It was not hard to fall asleep by nine, considering that we had to be up by five thirty the following morning. If you weren't on barn duty, then you had kitchen or bathroom duty, either of which I found considerably easier than smelling manure at such an early hour. Breakfast was huge, with pancakes and bacon, platters of scrambled eggs and toast, and plastic pitchers of Tang. The cook, Sandy, large-bosomed and big-bottomed in her tight T-shirt and shorts, called us to chow with a metal triangle, hung from a back tree under which there were two rickety wooden chairs for Liz and Ted, whom we called by their first names in an era when all children addressed adults as Mr. and Mrs.

The place was casual and dirty. Sherlock, the only dog allowed in the house, skulked around under the long trestle tables, hoping for the tidbits that always fell haphazardly and also were offered from the hands of the girls who fed him surreptitiously, despite the rules. He could have grown fat on such treats but instead frisked around the stalls and the riding rings, chasing the barn swallows, the cats, and the heels of the horses.

When my parents came for visiting days that first year, my mother always made a point of searching out Sherlock and, despite his size, held him on her lap to cuddle, his back legs dangling. I once had a photo, now lost to time and disorganization, of her with him up against her cheek. Both she and Joy talked incessantly about adopting him and taking him home. This was not to be, as he was well loved by the farm's owners, who would not consider placing him elsewhere because he was so sweet. I, too, was disappointed that Sherlock couldn't come with us.

Those visiting days were nevertheless reassuring to me: I could see my mother was all right. Sometimes there were shadows clinging to her, but other times she seemed cheerful enough to laugh at all our antics. Once she even perched atop Maxine's horse Xantippe, with her safari hat on her head. She and my dad inevitably came on the Saturdays when the farm hosted "shows" and there were classes galore: riders came from all around to compete in equitation on the flat, equitation over fences, hunter classes, and conformation. Every class had its ribbons, and no one won based on a judge's good humor or a desire to pass the ribbons around to each camper or to the numerous guests from the other camps. When you won, you won, and my parents applauded hard.

I decided I wanted to be involved with horses for the rest of my life and become a serious rider, and eventually a breeder, running a farm the way Liz and Ted did. When I failed geometry in the tenth grade, my mother lugged me over to her psychiatrist's office, where I explained that I intended to go into the horse business and would never need an ounce of mathematics. He smiled and advised me to keep my options open.

My mother continued to talk wistfully about adopting Sherlock and his funny, patched face. Sherlock was the runt of the litter and my mother loved runts, having considered herself one for the many years she believed she was the less favored child in her family. Even at Christmas, she voted for the smallest, most crooked tree in the lot. She was sure that Sherlock needed a home and that that home was ours.

four

IN 1966, WE TRADED in our old house in Newton for a new place in Weston, another Boston suburb. It came complete with a big kitchen and a mudroom specifically designed for dogs with wet feet. It was an upper-middle-class suburb, so it was a move into a better school system and what my parents saw as a "better neighborhood."

It was to this house that Penny soon arrived—toted in by Me-Me through an uncertain route. My sister, my father, and I were ecstatic, even though Penny was someone else's reject and had probably been abused. She was already a year old, and she ran away from the initial enthusiasm of Joy and me on her first day with us to vomit behind the shrubs lining the foundations of our spacious new home. Shy, tentative, and vulnerable, she initially trembled when we held her, as if waiting for the next kick in the ribs, and she was always afraid of men and brooms, leading us to speculate that perhaps a man with a long-handled object had abused her. Nevertheless, over time she became my father's special dog, and eventually she settled in to the idiosyncratic nature of the Sexton household.

I don't know how pleased my mother actually was at this new dog's arrival. At close to a year old, Penny was not as cute as a puppy. My mother was partial to puppies, even though she was the one supervising the house training. Penny wasn't a particularly pretty girl, either, with her eye trim an incomplete ring around the pink skin of her eye, instead of a proper thick black line. Her coat was sparsely spotted, and those spots that were there were not evenly distributed.

Penny had an annoying habit of whining endlessly, and it was often difficult not to spank her to shut her up. I remember feeling scandalized that I could even want to do such a thing, could feel such a way. But she was not the easy dog Clover had been. One day, with Penny left alone in the house for hours because my mother was once again in the hospital and my father was at work, I came home from school to find she had chewed off a corner of my father's prized zebra rug. He had shot the creature on an African safari in the late sixties and taken the pelt home with him to be displayed on the living room floor, something I would later come to feel was repulsive. I had not yet come to my bewilderment at how my father could kill some animals and love others. Back then, I could only imagine his wrath, and so I spanked her until my hand throbbed, until she growled at me with a glint in her eye and I drew back, afraid and astonished at both her and myself. I didn't know that I had that kind of anger in me— the kind that would allow me to beat (that's truly what it was), even if only with my hand. I left the room ashamed, and I never did it again. I was horrified at myself, at what in that instant I had become—perhaps, temporarily, a person not so unlike my father, with his love of dispatching beautiful animals with his gun.

Every evening, let out for her last potty of the night, Penny would often refuse to come back in, not even to the lure of a dog treat. She stood, just beyond reach, and taunted my tired father, who wanted only to go to bed. First Daddy would whistle, two beats. She would come within twenty feet and sit, tantalizingly, and wait. He'd whistle again and again. No movement. "Penny," he'd croon, "want a cookie?" Even that lure, the all-time bribe between human and canine, failed. Then she would shift just two feet forward, enough to make your heart rise with hope and then plummet when she stopped short.

"Cookie?"

And ten more feet.

"Good dog, good dog," didn't work either.

Eventually he would slam and lock the door against her, and she would sit whining under the porch light until I—my bedroom situated above the back door—would come down to let her in. And then the routine would begin again, with her just out of reach and me, now, begging her to come. At last, I would lock up again and go back to bed, this time with my head under the pillow.

It was up to Joy and me, young adolescents now, to teach Penny a few basic commands, like *sit* and *down* and *stay*. Though Clover had died on the road, once again the back door was always open—but Penny, fortunately, did not wander. We all relaxed, and the household melded together once again.

By this time, I had a firmly entrenched affection for dogs, for the way they set me free in love. There were no strings attached when dogs were the objects of your adoration. There was only loving aplenty coming back at you, even with the sometimes-frustrating Penny.

. . .

Raising Penny's litter was almost like being at Highlawn, and my mother's good mood persisted, perhaps urged on by the mewling from the basement that gradually grew into small barks. The puppies eventually graduated from nursing to eating a mush made of cream of wheat and milk from a baking pan, climbing in headfirst and emerging coated in sticky sludge on those first few days of experimentation—but ferociously licked clean by the other pups, if Penny didn't get there first. One by one, the pups were brought upstairs to the kitchen so that we could play with them, not knowing that we were actually doing something important: socializing them to loud noises and the busy activity of a family. My parents knew nothing at all about raising a litter and neglected to have their dewclaws removed early after birth—a small operation performed even more frequently these days, which saves a dog tearing off his useless vestigial fifth toe, up high on the front leg, later in life.

Although the opening of the puppies' eyes was followed closely by the opening of their ear canals at about three weeks, my parents also didn't know to test them for deafness—but Me-Me did, following them around with a pot and spoon and banging loudly to see which ones turned to the noise. Happily, all of them did. My parents and Me-Me knew nothing about what to do with deaf pups except to send them to farms, but they did get them their first shots before placing them in homes, charging $200 for each, an amount to which they now felt entitled, because though the pups had no papers, they were still purebreds.

We kept one from the litter, and Joy and I called her Gidget after our heroine Sally Field. We were still caught up in a whirl of canned television programs and frozen Saturday-night pizzas—not yet ready, as was so typical of the age back then, for boys and dates.

Gidget was one of the sweetest pups we would ever own. She was a beauty to look at, with evenly spaced spots and lovely, full ears. All her eye and nose trim were finished in the darkest black, and her eyes were a deep, deep brown. Her loving disposition led us all to adore her, though she bonded with Joy and me particularly. She seemed blessed with a halo of light, a lively dog, defying her mother's aloof temperament, and she followed us from room to room, stretching out at our feet with a satisfied groan. She was our first Dalmatian to smile since Clover, a trait common within the breed, by lifting her lips in a grin of happiness.

At the time she turned a year old, her fur began to turn patchy and fall out. We nicknamed her "the pink panther," for the pink-and-white patches that were invading her black-and-white spots.

However, after a while, it became a joke tinged with worry. Soon her skin became raw and oozing where she scratched at the itch relentlessly, but the vet was stymied about what to do. Eventually my father took her into the Angell Animal Medical Center in Boston for a consultation. We were given a variety of medications, none of which seemed to help for more than a month or two.

In June of that year, after we left for camp and while my parents were on their safari in Africa, Gidget and Penny both went into a boarding facility for a month. Why my grandmother didn't care for them I don't remember, but when she went to pick them up just before my parents' return, Gidget had no coat left at all. She was a walking bleeding sore. Nana marched off without paying the bill. My parents came home to find the house in an uproar.

Back to Angell Gidget went. Now my father was told she had a variety of mange that was heritable and incurable, passed along by Penny, who never should have been bred for this reason. Tiny mites got into the hair shafts of the coat and under the skin, causing an unbearable itch and the fur to fall out in handfuls. Dad was given a viscous brown solution to pour over her daily, so caustic he had to use rubber gloves.

In the tub Gidget sat immobile as a statue, stoically bearing the terrible scald of the medicated liquid. Where other dogs would have shaken, or tried to escape, she waited, taking on the pain gracefully. My father, the hunter, handled her extremely gently. I will never forget the sight of her there, poised under the spout, desperate for the relief of the cool water, but holding fast until my father turned on the faucets. She was a brave little pup. Dalmatians are nothing if not stubborn—but they are equally courageous—and little Gidget taught me a lot about bravery.

The treatments didn't work and the mange grew worse and worse, until she was a sorry mess of scabs. Eventually my father took her back to Angell, where he was told that there was nothing more to be done for her. On his own, he decided it was time. He held her in his arms as they gave her the needle, and only when she relaxed into death did he put her down on the table. He cried the whole way home in the car.

In this way I learned that you never leave an animal to die alone. It was one of the greatest lessons my father ever taught me.

It came as a terrible shock to Joy and me. Gidget had been there one minute, and the next—like a puff of smoke—gone. We all mourned. Penny remained. Though never as affectionate and lovely as her daughter, she was still a dog long in wisdom. She always let you know her limits, and she curled up most days in the same chair in my mother's writing room that had been Clover's so many years before. Though she didn't pad from room to room with you in companionable silence the way Gidget had, I nevertheless felt empathetic toward her because she came to us from a life that involved unhappiness, perhaps even some kind of trauma.

I believe that for my mother, all our dogs were "therapy dogs"—even though that concept did not yet exist in the general lexicon. She loved to stroke their soft coats; the motion mesmerized her and perhaps helped her bear her depression a bit. And so they were to us all: when my parents argued verbally, or fought physically, or when my mother danced with death, Joy and I could always retreat to a dog and hold on tight.

. . .

The loss of Gidget overshadowed our lives, and it was not long before we were ready to venture forth with another puppy. My mother's condition had also deteriorated. Her depression settled in again and attached itself like a cloak under which we were all suffocating. It was a dark time, marked with a loss of hope.

But another miracle was to come, specifically to my mother, but in turn, also to us. It was 1969, and the miracle's name was Daisy. Though my mother hadn't wanted the work of another dog, one evening my father simply came in the back door from the garage after work and called out to my mother, where she sat typing, "Anne, I've done something terrible."

"Did you crash the car?" She came running.

And just like that, he set down on the floor a small puppy with floppy spotted ears that felt like velvet and eyes that looked as if they had been rimmed with kohl. He told us how she had climbed out of her box on the passenger seat of the car and snuggled up into his lap, something like a cat, seeking his warmth. That action was to define her nature: Daisy always wanted to curl up around you. As affectionate as they come, perhaps even more so than Gidget.

Dad claimed that she was an anniversary gift for my mother. That night, as she became a part of our family, she left the kitchen to explore, waddled into my mother's writing room, and squatted in front of the fireplace to pee, as if claiming her territory. My mother's exasperated reaction was predictable.

Returning one night from dinner, my mother was struck with an idea in the dark of the car. In her play, *Mercy Street*, produced off Broadway in 1969, she had named her heroine Daisy, taken from a song called "Daisy Bell."

The name Daisy stuck, and ultimately my mother loved her as intensely as she loved her character. The puppy and the play had ushered in another era of a manic, upward swing into delight with life. Our family relaxed once again, undoubtedly because of my mother's improved outlook. And from then on, until the very day she died, each postcard and letter she wrote in response to a piece of fan mail was signed with a hand-drawn daisy.

With the advent of Daisy came the advent of joy.

She was shortly nicknamed Daisy-Do, and Daisy Doodle Bug, and proved to be what my father lovingly referred to as a goof bucket. Quick beyond anyone's expectations, she chased the cats from chair to chair and played hide-and-seek with whomever would pay attention to her. Often she could be seen perched atop the massive set of rocks in the front yard, where she stood guard over the house and barked at passersby.

She seemed to have a downright sense of humor, pleasing and sometimes surprising everyone who lived at 14 Black Oak Road, and those who visited as well.

Daisy loved to chase squirrels, mice, and any small animal that moved. Just like a cat, she would bring her trophies to the kitchen, dropping them at my father's feet with a mischievous expression on her face. One morning, she strutted in proudly, crossed to the stove where my father was frying up the bacon, and hawked up a whole squirrel, minus the tail, in one entire piece. Joy and I screamed and Dad was stuck with cleaning up the bloody mess. From then on, we all called her "The Trojan Dog."

But Daisy did have one fatal flaw that gave us deep anxiety: she loved to chase cars. My parents seemed oblivious to the fact that we now had a fully fenced backyard that easily could have solved the problem and instead kept letting her out the kitchen door that bordered on the road, where the cars moved past at a steady and regular clip.

One day, there was a shriek of brakes from the road, and Daisy came limping back home with one leg dangling, held uselessly off the ground. After a trip to the vet, her broken leg was set in a plaster cast from paw to elbow. My parents didn't seem particularly upset, though Joy and I were, and it was indicative of their distracted attitude that when the leg twisted in the cast, thus healing as crooked as a gnarly old tree limb, they did not take her back to the animal hospital to have the bone reset, but allowed her to hobble, however expertly, on the crippled leg. It was the kind of deformity that caused people to catch their breath when she limped up to them, tail wagging hard enough to bang into chairs and tables and knock over any drink within reach. It did seem to stop her from chasing cars, however, and perhaps that was my parents' collective unconscious speaking: they believed her deformity protected her. Her leg did keep her safe from the vehicles she only barked at now—but she was not safe forever.

It was an afternoon in October of 1975, a year following my mother's suicide, and there was a cool and welcome nip to the air after the two weeks of Indian summer that had just cleared out. The black oaks were flaming up in red and orange along the street, weaving their bright colors through the swamp maples out behind the house. I tried not to think about the fact that the weather and the aura of autumn had been just like this the afternoon of my mother's suicide only a year before.

My father, Joy, and I were painting the south wall of the living room in the house in Weston. There was much repair and maintenance work to be done, as my mother had let many things slide since she and my father divorced in 1972 and he moved out of the house.

As we painted we didn't talk much. There was a pleasant silence to it all, just the movement of our arms up and down and then the stretch into the bucket of white at our feet. The knock at the back door interrupted us, and it was Joy who went to answer. She came back quickly and her voice was alarmed.

"There's a woman out there who says she hit a black-and-white dog with her car."

We ran to the kitchen and crowded around the screen door.

"I'm so sorry," she said, looking as if she would cry. "I didn't mean to hit it, it ran out in front of my wheels."

"Where is she?" my father asked quickly.

"I don't know. It just ran off." She pointed in the direction of the wooded area across the street. "Somewhere over there."

My father nodded, and all three of us pushed past.

"Is there something I can do?" she called after us.

"Just go," my father said harshly, even though ordinarily he was scrupulously polite.

We searched the woods for over an hour and couldn't find her, returning home at last, discouraged and afraid, but it was a fear we couldn't admit to. My father went back to painting, Joy left with a boyfriend, and I took off with an old high school buddy. We couldn't bear waiting to see if Daisy would reappear.

There is a general disagreement between Joy and me about what happened next. She remembers that it was she, as she was returning home, who spotted Daisy out behind our house on the neighbor's property line. Yet somehow I can also see it, as sharply as if it were happening in this instant: I looked out the driver's window of my car as I came down Highland Street, scanning the trees in the back swamp, a painter's palette of orange and gold and red, their trunks virtually invisible. Only a flash of white stood out, stark against the riot of color, just for a moment.

The sisterly difference of opinion will never be resolved, but in any case, this was the point at which the two of us joined in the driveway and ran into the woods to the now-appropriate place. We found Daisy lying on her side, her legs outstretched, as if she had been running and just fallen in place.

"I'll go get Daddy," Joy said urgently, turning back.

I stayed, and reached out to touch Daisy. Under her soft coat, her flesh was like cold stone. I snatched my hand back, scalded as if by dry ice. I had never touched a dead body before. My mother's had been taken away by ambulance on the day she died, before I ever reached the house, and I had always wondered what it would have been like to have had the chance to say good-bye—a squeeze of the hand, or a kiss on the forehead.

I rocked back on my heels to get away.

As my father and Joy ran up, I started to cry.

Daddy gathered Daisy in his arms, and we took her around back, to a place behind the house where the ground was soft and yielding. He shoveled for what seemed like a long time, tears running down his face. Joy went back to the house for a blanket. Then we all stood, sobbing. The sounds we made were guttural and rough, but we were unable to stop. Daisy had been, without question, my mother's dog. And in this season of loss, we all now wept as if we were at my mother's memorial service once more.

Gently, Dad lifted Daisy up and then knelt to lay her down into the deep and wide hole. He covered her with the blanket. He picked up the shovel and began to move the soil back in on her. I turned away. I couldn't bear the sight of the dirt falling on her.

The box of my mother's ashes was in my father's bedroom closet, shoved to the back of a high shelf, yet never out of my mind. It had been a year and we still had not been able to bury her, not even in a private family service. Yet now, suddenly and without warning, we stood at a grave—bewildered, perhaps, because it was not hers. Not my father, not my sister, not I, had been able to manage the organization of the steps necessary to consign her to the ground. No dirt had yet been shoveled for her.

"It's as if Mom is dying all over again," said Joy.

When my father was done with the shovel and tamped the ground shut with his feet, we put our arms around each other and just stood there, exhausted. Not since the afternoon of the suicide had I felt so bleak. There were no miracles to be found that Saturday, and it would be a long time before I was willing to give my heart to another dog again.

PART II

our very own

Rhiannon

Tia

five

DURING THE YEARS AFTER college, my boyfriend and I lived in small apartments that forbade dogs. Fresh from Harvard, Jim Fiske and I set up shop in a small studio west of Boston, and I began work on what would be my first foray into the literary world, immersing myself in editing my mother's correspondence in *Anne Sexton: A Self-Portrait in Letters.* Hours unraveled in the Special Collections Library at Boston University, where her archive was housed at that time, and those long stretches away from home, as well as the fact that we had no room in our tiny apartment for a puppy, meant dog ownership was impossible. In any case, my heart had no room, for Daisy still filled it. It would be close to fifteen years later before I felt motivated to try again. Mom was gone, Daisy was gone: I didn't even want to begin to try to fill those particular voids.

The next four years were consumed by Jim's attendance at Harvard Medical School and by my first novel. Once again, we lived in a dog-unfriendly apartment building. I had to make do with frequent trips out to Weston, to visit the aging Penny, any time I wanted a dog fix. But, in truth, as the four years passed, I didn't think about dogs that much. My mind was on many other things, like work, and a relationship, and I had walled myself off from the trauma of two sudden deaths by refusing to even think of making myself so vulnerable again.

Marriage in 1979 brought new responsibilities and another small living space, this time in a Harvard dorm, where Jim and I became residential tutors to the undergrads as a way of saving money as he went to business school. Our schedules were full—I was writing my second novel and he was working. I found myself once again returning to my father's home as a way of getting my hands on a dog. Penny, old and arthritic, would still cuddle up on the nights I came for dinner. It made me sad: to see the final curtain falling on the line of the Sexton Dalmatians, as my father said he would not get another dog when she died. He had remarried, and his new wife wanted to travel.

Just before Jim and I moved to Manhattan for his new job on Wall Street, my father put Penny to sleep. His wife seemed relieved; my father was quietly heartbroken. I mourned in a distracted sort of way, as my life seemed to have spun beyond dogs, into the world of children.

It was to a concrete high-rise overlooking the East River that I brought my first child home from New York University Hospital. I had been on strict bed rest for eight months of the pregnancy but hadn't much minded, as I had had three previous miscarriages and would have done anything to make certain this baby survived. Yet, how I wished I had a therapy dog, those soft Dalmatian eyes to buffer me from the anxiety as the weeks rolled slowly by. In February of 1983, Nathaniel was born, followed shortly by Gabe in 1984.

When we moved the family to the suburb of Scarsdale, a forty-minute train ride outside of the city, it was the first time I allowed myself to again think seriously about getting a dog. We lived in a small brick house with three bedrooms, one that reminded me of the house in Newton Lower Falls where I had grown up. There was a very small yard in the back, with a two-foot-high fence, one possibly suitable for a cocker spaniel or a Chihuahua or some other toy-size dog—but definitely not for a Dalmatian.

Somehow I just couldn't get past it. A Dalmatian it had to be. We considered building a higher fence, but I knew the yard was just too small for the boundless energy of my favorite dog. And then, too, there were the demands of both my sons. Nathaniel was now nearly two and a curious, impossible toddler, and Gabe was still newborn, needing nursing and constant diaper changes. Perhaps inevitably, I found another sort of solution, a temporary one that sufficed for five years. An Abyssinian kitten bought on impulse when I went with a friend to a cattery to pick up her second Aby. As I watched the slinky red cats twine their way around our legs, the old yearning arose in me, and I called Jim. "How would you feel about a cat?" I asked, fooling myself into thinking that this would suffice.

He didn't sound enthused, having come from a home where no pets had been allowed, but he knew how much I craved a dog again, as I stopped to pet with longing every canine that came down the street. It seemed that we never saw Dalmatians. Had the breed become extinct? I wondered. Would I ever have again the special grin of a Dalmatian in my life?

The following Christmas the unexpected occurred. As a surprise for my sister, her husband arranged for a special sort of present, which was of course a Dalmatian puppy. As Daisy had been for our mother, Jenny also became a "therapy dog" of sorts, a comfort for both Joy and her husband, who were having trouble conceiving. For a time, Jenny was to be the recipient of the love they could not give to a newborn, and when their adopted daughter came into the family, their beloved Dal was loved by someone new.

I was filled with happiness for them but felt a sharp envy as well. When we first visited them in their home in Newton Lower Falls, only a few blocks from the house I had been raised in, I felt as if I were zooming back in a time machine. Not only was I in the place of my birth, but I was petting the dog of my childhood.

In 1989, the Fiske family left New York and followed a career shift for Jim to a suburb south of San Francisco. For the very first time in all those years since Daisy died, I had a house with a large, fenced yard. The yearning revved itself up. The cats (there were now two of them), beloved by all, nevertheless faded into the background. This was the moment I had been waiting for, and eleven years had been too long. And so it was that when the kids graduated from kindergarten to grammar school, I listened to their entreaties and my own inner longing. As they, now eight and six, began to beg for a dog, I was reminded of the way Joy and I had been similarly single-minded on the subject with my father. Once again, all the families around us, and all the children's friends, had dogs. But Jim was even more resistant than he had been with the acquisition of the cats.

Nevertheless, I called the American Kennel Club to find a Dalmatian breeder in our area. Without telling him. He had never before had a pet of any kind other than the Abyssinians,

Doppler and Caya. He had never known a minute of the kind of loving a dog would bring.

I called the four names the AKC gave me and then secretly mailed a deposit to the three who were soon to have litters. I wanted a girl. I knew the wait would be several months, or longer, for the harder-to-obtain females. In all my family years with Dals, we had never had anything but. I couldn't imagine breaking the streak with a boy.

Marty and Stu Stanford of StageCoach Dalmatians were the nearest to us. They didn't have any puppies available at the time and weren't expecting any for another six months, but Marty invited me to come over and meet her grown dogs, so that I could see her line and get on her list.

I don't know what I expected, but I didn't find a big kennel with a string of runs filled with barking dogs. StageCoach was simply the Stanford's home, a small ranch house even smaller than the Colonial I had grown up in, where we lived with Clover and Angel. Like all my childhood dogs, the Stanfords' were housedogs. They slept in heavy-duty plastic crates stacked one on top of the other in the kitchen next to the oven. I looked at those crates with misgivings, thinking that they were a cruel alternative to letting your dog roam through the house. But—I reminded myself—not the street.

Yet, when we went into the backyard with its six-foot fence, five dogs were running around quite freely: three females and two males. The girls were a mother and her two daughters. The mother was now spayed but had been a noted champion. The Stanfords were waiting to breed one of the daughters, also a champion, at her next season. I had my deposit riding on that litter, perhaps six months hence, though there was no guarantee she would get pregnant, or that a girl would be available.

Or that I'd be able to discipline myself to wait six months. I reminded myself that I had other breeders to meet, and some of them had litters due sooner.

The Stanford's youngest girl, Rhiannon, now over a year old, was just starting out in the show ring. Marty and Stu were looking for a "show home" for her now because they believed it would be best for her if she moved out from under her mother's shadow. They felt she might be excellent material for a beginner to train and exhibit on the days when neither of them was available. They would co-own the dog with her new owner and continue to show her in the extremely competitive California circuit. This seemed an interesting concept, one I had never heard of before.

She had been named after a Welsh witch and, of course, after the Fleetwood Mac song. She had a lot of spots, and many of them were run together in long wavy lines—a very "colorful" dog, as Dalmatian breeders kindly put it. Her eyes were light brown (a minor fault, though I couldn't have known that then), but more important than their color was the soulful look she gave me as she came right over and put her head in my lap. Her whiskers prickled the skin of my leg. I stroked her silky head. Rapture.

When I left that day, I was totally smitten by each dog, even those who were so busy playing that they paid me little mind. All I could think about was when a pup would be available. All the fear and grief I had held when Daisy died had been long since resolved. I was ready.

And my boys were, too. When I got home, Nathaniel pestered me with questions and Gabe begged to go over to the Stanfords' the next day so that they could meet the dogs. I called again and got permission to bring them. Still I mentioned nothing to Jim. As we went through the backyard gate, the dogs ran up, barking and smiling. The boys initially thought those grins were snarls and drew back. I had to explain it was the breed's way of being submissive and happy.

Together, they all ran on the lawn as Marty and I talked more about the kind of home Dalmatians needed, as if I didn't know: consistent, disciplined, with plenty of exercise and a lot of hands-on love. They were not the kind of dog you could confine to a kennel run in the backyard and walk away from. Not unless you wanted a lot of barking and digging and other destructive behaviors. They were true companion dogs. Once again, unbidden, Rhiannon came over and put her head in my lap.

"Looks like she's picked you out," Marty commented.

I laughed. "Maybe I should take her instead of waiting for a pup."

"Maybe you should," Marty answered, ever the businesswoman, sensing an opportunity. Her wide freckled face was so friendly and open. It was easy to feel as if we had known each other for years.

I paused and looked down at my lap. The weight of Rhiannon's head on my knee was sweet. The Stanfords would show her; I would love her.

But I pushed the thought away. I wanted a puppy, I reiterated to myself, an affectionate puppy I could raise from the get-go as all mine, not a yearling who had been at the bottom of the pack for the first twelve months of her life, overshadowed by both mother and sister.

Yet, without realizing it, I once again identified with the underdog, just as I had with Sherlock and his deafness, just as I had with Penny and her early difficulties. Dim in the bright light of my mother's dramatic talent and her ever-present mental illness, my sister and I had often been shoved to one side as well. Now it was Rhiannon who lived in the shadows. Suddenly all I could think of was rescuing her and making her someone's top dog.

Startled, I realized that I had made up my mind, and as I drove home, I pondered a new problem: how to convince Jim that it was time for a dog. I didn't relish the possibility of an argument.

Later that afternoon, back at home, the children were distracted from their homework. "Why couldn't we just get Rhiannon today?" asked Nathaniel.

"Rhiannon," Gabe chimed in. "Tomorrow."

"We'll see," I comforted them. "We have to talk to Daddy first."

We went out to dinner that night, meeting Jim at Scott's, a seafood restaurant near his office. It took only a moment before the kids were babbling about the dog. He started to frown.

"You took them to see a breeder without even asking me how I felt about a dog?" He gave me an angry glance.

I sighed. I hadn't asked him about a dog because I didn't want to hear him say no. I knew it was wrong.

At this point I wanted to give Rhiannon a home. I had become committed to creating a place where she could be number one.

"Please!" Nathaniel begged.

"Oh, Daddy, come on!" entreated Gabe.

"As usual, I'd look like the bad guy," he groused, rumpling his hair with his hand.

"You don't have to." I smiled at him winningly.

"I thought you wanted a puppy. This is a dog."

I bit my lip. I didn't know quite how to explain why I had changed my mind.

He smiled then, just a little bit, as if he didn't really want me to see.

The next day I went out and purchased the recommended crate and a leash, a big bed and a pooper-scooper. Rhiannon came home to stay.

six

RHIANNON'S ATTACHMENT TO ME was as strong as steel. She followed me from room to room and always slept curled up at my feet as I worked in my office at the computer, except for the times when I left the house and she slept happily in her crate, which was as secure a den for her as it had been at the Stanfords.' I was learning.

Plainly put, she adored me—the one who had rescued her from being at the bottom of the pack and moved her up to being a prized top dog—and I adored her back in equal measure. Over time, I began to realize she was a "special" dog, the kind that intuited all my emotions, wrapped herself around me in a cocoon of devotion and loyalty, and stepped up to deliver whatever I required of her.

As the only dog in the house, she received a deluge of affection from the boys as well. Even my father, when he came from Boston for a visit, fell in love with Rhiannon and her gentle ways. One year, he brought her a gift and left it till last on Christmas morning, stuffed into her stocking, deliciously anticipating her reaction. When he pulled it out and unwrapped it for her, he looked very satisfied with himself and handed over a dog bone the size of a dinosaur's leg. Rhiannon picked it up in her mouth and then just stood there, as if puzzled as to what to do with it. We all erupted into laughter as she set it down on the floor gingerly and waited for someone to tell her what came next.

Jim learned to love Rhiannon, tentatively at first and then with a sort of distracted affection. After I went to bed, she often sat under his desk as he worked in the bedroom late into the evening, warming his toes by resting her muzzle across them. That cozy situation lasted until the night he was immersed enough in his computer not to note her insistent whining to go out, and she peed on his feet. Where I would have shrugged it off, figuring such an event was just part of being a dog owner, he then banished her from the cubbyhole. Jim loved Rhiannon but perhaps never felt truly bonded to her, not with that solid sense of communion the kids and I felt. While he grew to be a dog lover, he would never be a dog person.

• • •

The arrival of Rhiannon ushered in a whole new decade for me. Since we had moved to California, I had had the friendships created when Jim and I went to business dinners or his company's annual outings and Christmas parties, or when we met our new California neighbors at Fourth of July parades, or when one of the kids made friends with a schoolmate and I spent time with the mother on the edge of the soccer field. But I missed all my close friends—mostly those from college years—who had remained behind when I moved to the West Coast. I was lonely for the kind of friendship that was independent of Jim or the kids.

And so I began, a little bit at a time, to involve myself in the hobby of showing dogs, making new friendships as I went along. Rhiannon had helped me to find an activity created solely for me. My family provided a positive backdrop, cheering me on as I pursued It. This reminded me of days at Highlawn, of the dusty ring where we all rode our hearts out, of the excitement of competing and winning a ribbon or a trophy.

By 1992, I had joined the Dalmatian Club of Northern California and the Dalmatian Club of America. Jim had no interest, but he was happy to see me with an activity that made me feel great and anchored my days around more than kids and work and the depression that I still fought intermittently.

He was even starting to enjoy watching the kids on his own—more than when I had been home full-time on the weekends—as he could choose activities for them that he really enjoyed, too, like tennis and baseball, sports that didn't interest me much. Soon I was addicted to "show and go," which was the term for driving hours to a show at a distant venue, being in the ring for all of ten minutes, and then, sometimes defeated, turning around to go home again—all without having hung around the fairgrounds for more than an hour or two.

Eventually I would make many "dog" friends, and it was like unraveling a daisy chain of people and their kennels—if you knew one breeder, they introduced you to the next, and over time you knew the people at Paisley and Spotlight and St. Florian and Driftwood and Brookside and Blackberry. It was amazing to me how welcoming everyone was when all they knew about you was that you loved Dals.

But at first there had simply been Marty Stanford, who did almost all the showing, and Stu, extremely personable and adored by almost everyone on the Dal circuit. Initially, I'd tagged along with Marty to every show she entered and helped clean up the dogs before their classes.

That meant I did much of the dirty work: getting the dogs ready well in advance of their ring time, clipping the edges of their coats and their whiskers, washing them down with Self Rinse, and applying the forbidden chalk to those yellowed areas, like the hocks and feet, that were stained and needed to be smoothed over. And then, before entering the ring, there was the final potty run, with its requisite smelly, heavy baggie. It wasn't long before others who knew her began to observe that Marty had a new "bucket bitch."

I resented the term—but not enough to quit the role. Instead, I vowed to show my own dogs someday. No co-owning for me again. I felt as if I were paying my dues by helping Marty, and in return had the opportunity to hang around ringside and hear what others breeders were discussing, often behind their hands. Competition was stiff and gossip rampant. Showing was sometimes extremely political, with well-established, highly visible breeders or professional handlers winning most of the points, especially in the "Group" rings. In "Groups" (of which there were seven: Sporting, Hound, Working, Terrier, Toy, Non-Sporting, Herding), the Best-of-Breed winners competed against the others, and then only the single winner from each of the Groups went on to compete for the top honor, Best in Show.

I found myself anticipating each show day eagerly. Watching the animals move fluidly through their paces, or stand up proudly for the judge's examination, was a recalled pleasure. As my critical eye developed, I could increasingly determine which dogs were, though sometimes serendipitously, worthy of a ribbon.

What I liked the best, however, was the chance to work with the dogs, croon in their ears as I brushed their perennially shedding coats with the same kind of curry comb I'd used at summer camp.

. . .

Marty Stanford introduced me to Kathryn Blink, and we turned into good friends quite quickly. I had not stopped hankering after a pup even after Rhiannon moved in, and I had made Jim promise me that we could have one more dog. By the time Kathryn and I got to be close, my family was at the top of her list for a litter that had just been born.

She was a breeder of equal reputation to Marty and Stu, or perhaps greater, and Driftwood Farm, just one town away from me, was known for its obedience dogs as well as its breed-ring champions. Kathryn had a good sense of humor and was known for her loud laugh and bossy manner. I was drawn to her sense of buoyancy, which was refreshing after all of Marty's seriousness, but especially because she treated me as an equal, not as a daughter.

And through Kathryn, I met Dawn Mauel of Saint Florian Dalmatians, well respected for her line as well as her expert handling. She wasn't interested in obedience, but that didn't seem to stop a friendship from developing between us. Per-haps I was just glad not to have someone to compete with in that arena. Short, with a head of thick, glossy black hair, she was very attractive, and I always felt a bit at a disadvantage when standing next to her, a gangly blonde Jeff to her petite dark Mutt. Over the next several years the friendship deepened until it became the one I depended on and enjoyed the most. My world within the fancy was growing.

. . .

In January of 1993, I finally chose that puppy I'd been looking for, but this time, it was from one of Kathryn's litters. Born on December 30, Tia became an official family member that February. She was one of the smaller girls in the litter, and when I brought her home at eight weeks old, everyone loved her right away—including two-year-old Rhiannon. She was the prettiest Dalmatian I had ever owned, with just the right amount of "hand-painted" spotting, a lovely head shape, and dark brown eyes that made Rhiannon's look even lighter.

The dogs were, through a twist of pedigree, aunt and niece. Tia was a joyous pup, not unlike Daisy, with a Dalmatian smile for everyone and an independent streak that often led her into interesting predicaments. She loved to roll in the mud and come out coated black all the way up to her eyeballs. Her favorite spot to hang out was not a chair in my writing room, but underneath the wheelbarrow in the garden. I have many photos of her nestled in the grass with just her snoot peeking out around the wheels, garden tools mingled with old dog toys that obviously held no interest for her. Later we would discover what did hold her interest.

She quickly became enmeshed in the household. As she grew from puppyhood to adolescence, she became the star of the stories I told to the boys at bedtime. In addition to reading books to them, I made up fantasy tales in which Tia was a nightrider, encountering dragons and unicorns, wearing a ruby jewel in her forehead as a sign of her intrepid nature. Night by night she made her way from one land to another, up mountains and through forests, our independent voyager.

While Rhiannon was clearly my dog, Tia was everyone's dog. Whining wasn't part of her canine vocabulary, and she would just wait patiently until someone let her out the door or filled her dish with kibble. As our family ate dinner at the kitchen table, she hunkered down at our feet, waiting quietly for a piece of food to fall, rather than persistently nudging your elbow hard, as did Rhiannon.

Tia did have one unique trait, however, and as she grew, it turned into one of her main activities: despite the fact that Dals are not ratters, Tia loved to chase down squirrels, just as Daisy had. Rhiannon had never shown the slightest interest in a bird, snake, or squirrel, but Tia was wild for the latter, though she'd never actually caught one. Because this was safer than chasing cars, I didn't worry about it. Squirrels were too quick, though we found lots of trophies, usually dead roof rats (a California specialty), laid carefully at any one of our doorsteps.

With a curious streak built into her personality, Tia just couldn't keep from investigating things. One night just as I was turning out the light, I heard a loud scrabbling at the screen slider that led from our bedroom out into the backyard. As I walked to the door, the scratching grew more and more frantic, accompanied by moans. I opened to door to find Tia with the left side of her face covered in some kind of viscous glop. It was oozing right down into her eye and from there onto her muzzle and from there onto the rug. As I hollered at Jim to get a towel, I got my first whiff.

I had always imagined a skunk's spray to be more like the mist from an aerosol can. This was thick enough to scrape off with a spoon. I picked her up and ran with her to the bathroom, where I put her into the tub and turned the spray nozzle of cold water directly into her eyes. All I could think was that she might go blind. She stood there as bravely as Gidget once had and didn't move, letting the water flush the stuff out.

Jim was dispatched to Safeway to buy tomato juice. I was still rinsing Tia with cold water when he came back with four cans of tomato juice and three jugs of V8. He'd also brought vinegar because the checker at the store had sworn that vinegar was excellent at getting skunk out of dogs. I didn't know then about the sure-fire remedy for skunk that consisted of baking soda, hydrogen peroxide, and dishwashing soap.

Predictably enough, neither the tomato juice, nor the V8, nor the vinegar worked. The house stunk, she stunk, we stunk.

For the next six months, every time it rained and her coat got wet, it smelled like an invasion again, even though she had been sprayed only the one time. It finally occurred to us that from the position and quantity of slimy deposit on her, she must have been virtually sniffing his tail when he let go full in her face. She hadn't even had the time to turn aside.

Tia also liked to chase our two Abyssinian cats, who probably looked like red squirrels to her. As a small puppy, she began by wanting to romp gently after them, around and over the furniture, and I quickly grew exasperated at having to pick up family photos knocked from the piano top and chairs tipped over on their sides. Eventually the cats were relegated to the boy's end of the house and the family room, and the dogs took over the kitchen, living room, our bedroom, and my office.

One summer morning, Tia paced back and forth in front of the screen door in our bedroom, obviously highly anxious to go out, but—remembering the episode with the skunk—I hesitated and peered out into the yard. Nothing visible, I decided, reminding myself that skunks were nocturnal. Still, it was with some hesitation that I released her. Once I'd closed the slider behind her, however, I could see something was going on: she took off as if propelled from a cannon, tried to jump clear across the upper end of the swimming pool and fell in, clambered out by going up the steps she remembered so well, and then didn't pause a minute for even a shake—just started running again pell-mell across the yard, where she came face-to-face with a big bushy-tailed black squirrel.

Trapped, the squirrel ran in circles as Tia chased it, making the tragic mistake of not climbing the fence, which would have put it out of her reach. She was extremely fast, and it took her only a moment to pounce. I ran toward her, yelling at her to drop it, but quickly she shook her head sharply from side to side.

I arrived at her side, panting from my quick sprint, and she dropped it from her mouth. I grabbed her collar, slippery from her dunk in the pool. The squirrel was still alive, but with its neck broken, now paralyzed, looking up at us with one eye as it lay there on its side. There was not a mark on it, but it was clear it was checking out on life. Tia strained to be released, undoubtedly wanting to finish it off. I thought, in horror, that if I didn't let her go, I would have to kill it. I couldn't just leave it there to die, and I wasn't about to let her at it again. Angrily, I dragged my soaking-wet dog off to shut her in the garbage area. Once again, because she was wet, she stunk of skunk. I got a shovel and gave the squirrel a big bang on the head, then picked it up and took it out to the trash.

Tia was waiting for me. As I dumped my sad burden into the black can and locked the lid, I looked down at her, ready to begin the "bad dog!!" routine. But there she was: little Tia, joyous little Tia—who would have known there was a killer in her? She was wagging her tail as hard as she could, her whole body moving side to side. Her bright eyes shone up at me. I shut my mouth and went in for a bath towel.

One cool summer evening, the entire family was out in the backyard. As the sun went down, the boys and Jim were playing catch, and Rhiannon and I were working over white jumps on the lawn. We were getting ready to compete for the first leg of her first obedience title, at the Dalmatian Club of America National Specialty, the biggest annual show devoted solely to Dalmatians, which this year was to be held in San Rafael, just over the Golden Gate Bridge from where we lived. Tia began chasing the boys' ball and getting in the way.

In 1992, just about the time Tia arrived and I got a new prospect for the breed ring, I had switched gears from the conformation ring with Rhiannon and begun to train her for obedience as well. Here she would be judged on her performance at a certain set of tasks. As we practiced, slowly, several times a day, heeling smoothly and in concert as if we were one, her eyes were always on my face as we executed this pas de deux. I felt a surge of satisfaction. Loyal as ever, Rhiannon was eager to please me. It was a new sort of lesson: a dog's loyalty easily rivaled a human's. Kathryn and her obedience girl, Button, met up with Rhiannon and me several times a week to practice on the smooth surface of our backyard lawn.

Rhiannon turned out to have the kind of obedience potential that makes a handler wait to show her until perfection is achieved. No settling for scores of 175 out of a possible, but perhaps unattainable, 200. I wanted to see the high 190s, and I absolutely believed we could do it. Even the prestigious and coveted obedience award of what is commonly known as "High in Trial"—won by the dog with the top score overall and similar to conformation's Best in Show—might not be beyound her reach.

Ignoring Jim's problems as Tia continued to interfere with their ball that night, I put Rhiannon on a down stay and walked away from her, to go and hide behind a tree. For the Companion Dog obedience title (CD), it wasn't necessary for her to be going over the jumps or for me to be out of sight on a down stay, but she did have to remain lying on her side without changing position for a total of three minutes while I stood on the other side of the ring. I was training her with the requirements for the higher-level Companion Dog Excellent (CDX), as a way of making her truly solid for the CD we were working toward, and so I was asking her to stay without moving for five minutes.

"Come on boys, we're going in to read," Jim declared after a while, wiping his forehead on his sleeve. "I'm exhausted." Tia tagged after them, probably confident of cadging a scrap of whatever snack they would choose as they sat down with their books.

After I released her from her down stay, Rhiannon and I began heeling, moving up and down, back and forth, as a synchronized team. I called a pattern aloud the way the judge would, in any order he or she chose, in three short weeks. "Forward," then "right turn," then "fast," then "normal," then "left turn," then "slow," then "normal," then "about turn," then "halt." And at last, "Exercise finished!" Rhiannon had to watch my face the entire time even though she was at my side, to move with my every move. I wasn't satisfied with anything less than straight lines, good footwork, and smooth turns. Sometimes I used a clear Plexiglas rod to gently tap her butt or chest if she lagged behind or forged ahead a bit. I was back to showing again, with dogs rather than horses, and I was pursuing it with a vengeance. My family was proud and sometimes stood at the edge of the lawn to watch us practice.

I had begun by showing Rhiannon in the conformation ring, where classes are judged solely on the way the dog is put together structurally, the size and clarity of the spots, the motion of the body while moving around the ring; however, by the time she was three, I had come to the conclusion that the real reason Marty and Stu had placed her in a co-own home (perhaps without even acknowledging it to themselves) was because they wanted to fill her crate in their kitchen with a dog that had more potential. Rhiannon wasn't truly competitive in the conformation ring: she was too colorful; she was too high in the rear, too upright in the shoulder; her eyes were light enough to brighten a dark room; and she had long feet shaped like a rabbit's, rather than those resembling tight round cat's paws. She did have some good qualities, but not enough of them. Tia, on the other hand, was a different story. She had promise, and I was just beginning to show her in the "nine-to-twelve-month puppy bitch" class.

Though I had used to make fun of dog shows before I took Rhiannon from Marty and Stu, with the animals posed in stances and trotting around the ring, my new experiences had demonstrated that there was a whole science to it that many people just didn't understand. While often thought of as a beauty pageant, dog showing in the conformation ring is not that unlike a sporting event, such as horse show competitions at the upper levels where there are money trophies—and no one laughs at that. This competitive "fancy" takes into account, solely, the work for which the dog was originally bred, even though most dogs are no longer required to perform in this way. Each of the different breeds—from cockers to poodles to Irish setters—have certain physical and character requirements that enable him to hunt a fox, or to tree a badger, or to flush a covey of quail, or to dig a badger out of its burrow.

For the Dalmatian, originally a "coaching" dog that had to

run many miles—often fifteen to twenty daily, in the traces just behind the horses' hooves as they pulled a carriage—this meant he needed a strong and level top line coupled with the good angulation front and back that would produce an easy drive, a smooth and fluid motion built for endurance. A capacious chest was requisite so that the dog could breathe deeply for long periods of time, and his feet needed to be well padded and tight, ready for the rough roads and many miles he traveled.

Because the carriage took its passengers from inn to inn, he also served as a guard dog, protecting both the coach and its travelers. He was to bark at strangers, but never to attack, to warn off those who did not belong and alert those who did. It was only after horse-drawn fire engines made their debut that Dals became better known as firehouse mascots.

Naturally, Dals had to have a strong affinity for horses. Enter Sherlock. Enter "road trial" competitions, where the dogs work side by side with the horse, heeling at the rider's side, over miles of rough terrain—another sort of sport in which Dalmatians participate.

There was also the requirement that set the Dal apart from all other breeds: his spots. They were to range in size between a quarter and a dime, and were to be separate and well distributed. This was the only "cosmetic" requirement for the dog, but nevertheless an important one, for without it, the breeding pool could be altered by the inclusion of other dogs that did not share the traits so essential to a coach dog. Although not widely known, there are actually two kinds of Dalmatians—some with black spots and some with deeply colored chocolate spots, and with hazel eyes rather than the more common brown. This latter variety is called "liver." The liver gene is recessive, and so livers are more highly prized by some due to their comparative rarity.

And it was all these qualities, taken into consideration on a percentage basis, which decreed a winner in the breed ring. Rhiannon and her less-than-perfect show qualities had been my introduction into the world not only of dog showing, but also of dog breeding. Nevertheless, even if Marty and Stu had told me she wasn't truly a show dog, I would still have taken her because the boys and I had so badly wanted a dog to complete our family, just as Clover, Penny, Gidget, and Daisy had completed the family at Black Oak Road.

I had begun to handle Rhiannon in the ring myself after a year, because Marty soon had a new puppy who was a better candidate and she became too busy and distracted. I discovered I wanted to participate in the ring more often, even though it was rare for Rhiannon and me to win. The show bug had bitten me again, but my dog wasn't ideal: forget "going to Westminster," as friends not in the know sometimes suggested; it was in question whether she would ever become a champion. Tia would become my new opportunity in conformation.

• • •

The odds in the ring were often stacked against the new and the barely visible—like me. There were the politics of showing: well-known breeders, whom judges had seen in the ring for many years, and well-known handlers, whom judges had observed handling dogs to perfection since they had first come onto the scene, often did most of the winning.

Sometimes handlers arrived late to the ring because they had too many dogs to handle and were dashing from one class to another. Sometimes they even rode bikes back and forth from one ring to another, arriving to take from an assistant the dog who had been groomed to the nines and was waiting for the handoff.

Once, at Marty's insistence and in hopes of getting some points on Rhiannon, I hired Allyn Adair, a nationally known handler seen on television every year at Westminster with one of the top winning specials in the country. That particular day, I got more and more nervous as Dalmatian judging began. Rhiannon's class approached, and there was no sign of either Allyn or my dog. I had thought if he were going to be detained, there would at least be an assistant holding her ringside, ready to hand her off to Allyn. But I tried to calm myself, thinking of the many tales of Allyn's arriving late—one in particular when he'd taken off from the show grounds to go and buy a new pair of shoes and barely made it back in time. But legend had it that he'd never missed one yet. I reminded myself of all this as the males entered the ring, as it was customary that they go first and the bitches shortly followed thereafter.

I had been told many times never to question a handler, especially one you were paying top dollar, lest they cross you off their list (it was obvious who wielded the power in this relationship), but as the females began to file in, I ran back to the grooming area to discover Allyn sitting atop Rhiannon's crate eating a powdered donut. "They're in the ring," I cried in distress.

"*Dogs* are in the ring," he corrected me, laconically.

"*Bitches* are in the ring!" I responded, with temper.

He craned his head in the appropriate direction and was up in a flash. With all the white sugar on his suit, he looked like he'd walked through a blizzard of cocaine. Wiping himself down as he hustled Rhiannon out of her crate, he got her over to the ring after the "ring gate was closed." I was furious.

Handlers were the only ones always asking for late admittance, and most of the time, they were granted such, at the judge's discretion, because they were politically visible and because they were often flying from one ring to the next. Everyone groused about it, but no one did anything. There were certain things that were immutable at dog shows: if you didn't like them, I was told, don't show. It was a hard lesson for me—always so bent on fairness. Soon I lost that sense and just accepted the norm.

Allyn made it just in time to slide into line before the judge went over the dog in front of him—the only requirement for a late admission—but at that point, Rhiannon was too rattled to do much beside stand there with her head down. I never used Allyn again.

One afternoon, after coming in second to a dog I thought not as worthy as Rhiannon, I petulantly stripped off my armband number and tossed my red ribbon into a trash can beside the ring. Arriving back to the ringside chair, a friend gave me a look. "You could get sanctioned by the AKC for poor sportsmanship!" she cautioned, like a mother, and I resented this, even as I saw the truth in it.

It reminded me of what I had learned as a child, after a jumper's class I'd entered at Highlawn Farm: having fallen off my horse during the round over the fences, I threw my riding crop in my mother's lap and stalked off as I exited the ring. Thirty-some-odd years later, and I was still learning the same lesson.

I sat down with a sigh, Rhiannon at my knees, just in time to hear my number called out, as I had forgotten that I might need to go back into the ring for Reserve, always a possibility when the dog who beats you goes Winners—all part of a complicated system with which even dog show people sometimes have trouble keeping track. In a rush, I scrambled over to the trash can and began digging through the garbage as I looked for my paper number with its elastic band.

I began to draw away from Marty, wanting to be out on my own, and slowly I developed tighter relationships with new friends like Kathryn and Dawn. I had also begun to believe in myself as a handler. In spite of my weekly handling class, I still made mistakes, but I was eager and continued to try to show in both rings once I had picked up obedience. Despite all this, when Rhiannon and I failed to gather enough points to finish her championship, I began to resent that she had been sold to me as a viable show dog, when clearly she lacked both the aptitude and the qualities to do any real winning. Still, I wouldn't have traded her for the most beautiful dog in the breed ring. She never stopped trying, and when it came to obedience, she excelled—drawing on her relationship with me to develop an extremely focused attitude—perhaps the single most important quality it takes to become a champion obedience dog. It wasn't much longer before I began to rely solely on my new friends, all of whom were Dalmatian people.

seven

IN SAN RAFAEL, THE afternoon before the first day of the National had true Bay Area summer weather: the sky blue from horizon to horizon, the late sun gentle without being hot. As Dawn and I pulled up in my minivan to the show grounds, a breeze puffed and lifted the corners of the white tents that had been erected up and down on the grass, running alongside the rings that had been marked off with white chains. At this particular venue, the designated squares of green were carefully mowed and tended, and the rings were likely to be smooth and without too many holes that could trip up either dog or handler.

In the adjacent parking lot, the large recreational vehicle slots were already beginning to fill up. From forty-five-foot "buses" to the smaller trailers that were pulled behind cars, nearly all of them had awnings under which fellow Dal addicts could congregate out of the sun. As people set up their tents, they grouped themselves as near friends as possible; it was a nomadic tribe dominated by intricate relationships that rivaled those of the campers at Highlawn Farm.

It was the Dalmatian Club of Northern California's turn in the rotation to host the National Specialty, and as always, we had also worked out a special rate with the most decent hotel that would accept canines, the Embassy Suites in San Rafael. It was the first time the hotel had ever signed on for a dog "event." As we surveyed the lobby's furnishings and atmosphere, Dawn and I remarked that the hotel didn't know what they had gotten themselves into.

At the National, the only kind of dogs shown was Dals, and the classes stretched out a full five days including the Regional. The competition for Best of Breed took an entire day all by itself, sometimes with upward of over a hundred champion dogs entered, and then there were all the lesser classes, including the prestigious Futurity, where puppies were shown, solely by their breeders, as the future exemplars of the breed. First an upcoming litter had to be nominated before the bitch's due date, and then individual puppies had to be nominated before the pup was four months old. Everyone wanted to win this class, which was second only to Best in Specialty Show.

After the fourth day of the National, DCNC (as our club was known) would host its own specialty, still devoted solely to the Dalmatian. Other guests at the hotel would follow us with their eyes wide: most people had never seen so many Dalmatians in one place.

I was nervous, certain that there was so much Rhiannon and I could have worked harder on, so much more proofing we could have done to be certain that she wouldn't break on her downs or lag on her heeling. But I calmed myself, thinking that I didn't want to be like another friend who never seemed to take her dog into the ring because she was such a perfectionist.

• • •

Dawn and I often shared expenses in cheap motels, gas, mileage, and sometimes even food, depending on how strapped we were feeling. We spent many hours on the road, driving from California to Portland, California to Seattle, California to Denver, California to Arizona, from Northern California to Southern, across the country in her white minivan or my green "Dalopy." My van had been nicknamed by Jim—a jalopy for Dals. The trips were always filled with raucous laughter about ourselves, our competitors, our dogs—even our sex lives or what we thought of men in general. Hilarious girl talk, something I hadn't experienced much of in my all-too-serious and sensitive past as a child.

My own family of Jim, Nathaniel, and Gabe seemed very far away, far away from all the responsibilities that went along with being a wife and mother—and, much to my surprise, it felt good to be taking this break. I still called home every night, but I had to remind myself to do it, as the pace at the National was quick.

• • •

It was past five o'clock when we finally finished our unpacking, and though I was dying for a drink at the bar, we had to feed and potty the dogs first.

By then I had learned the trick of walking two dogs at a time without wrapping myself around trees and bushes, or falling off the curb. The dogs watered the bushes.

At last, Rhiannon and Tia and Dawn's Basha and Davenport were tucked safely in their boxes. The room had remained at 83 degrees, and I checked the air conditioner only to find that

it was still blowing warm air. I reported this to the front desk
when we went downstairs, expecting that they could fix it by
the time we were back from dinner, but they told me the repair
engineer wouldn't be in until the next morning. We resigned
ourselves to a hot night tossing on our shared double bed.

We put on our lipstick, donned our Dalmatian "garb" for the
Welcome Party, and made our way down to the bar, where the
horde of other dog owners had already claimed the entire place
for their own and were well on their way to getting sauced.

Nearly everyone was from somewhere else. Minneapolis and
Denver, Boston and D.C.—anyone who owned a show Dalmatian came to the National Specialty, complete with various
accents and different sorts of clothes, from string ties to sun-
dresses. I didn't know it then, but I was becoming part of a big
new family, another one dedicated solely to Dalmatians.

There was always a lot of interclub competition for the social
end of things year to year, and activities ranged from a BBQ
(for the West Coast clubs) to picnics (the East and the South),
and all manner of other things in between. In those years, none
of them were particularly original, especially the food (usually hamburgers or hot dogs and store-bought coleslaw), but
they all had something special attached to them. The Welcome
Party, often given at the hotel bar or a private room, always had
a theme: this time everyone was to dress in Dalmatian finery of
some kind, and it didn't matter if it was denim or diamonds. I
had on a denim jacket made from a pair of upside-down jeans
with a huge Dalmatian face, which was really the backside of
the pants, embroidered front and center across my back.

With nothing to eat but a few carrot sticks and a handful of
nuts, there was only booze—Dal owners were happy, and sometimes downright enthusiastic, drinkers—and this event had

these few key aspects of an Irish wake, except for lots of shouts floating across the press of bodies in tightly clustered groups— good natured clowning around as old-time friends reunited with those they hadn't seen since the last year's National.

There were people who'd been coming for fifty years, or more, as well as newcomers. Some of these breeders had kennels that had been in existence for decades, and some were just starting out, using all the tomfoolery to get to know people, barhopping and glad-handing in an attempt to learn names, make new friends, and develop contacts. In some ways it was similar to the business junkets Jim went on when he was away: have fun, but work on those business contacts as well.

There were all kinds of people in different situations: those who couldn't afford the hotel and lived out of their overstuffed cars like vagabonds; those wealthy enough to drive in style in their enormous RVs; those who bunked four to a room to economize, fighting over bathroom space; those who had their own rooms and didn't have to share anything at all. There were more overweight women than you could find at a Jenny Craig convention, many dressed egregiously— and quite a number of gay men, who sometimes flounced around the ring in gaudy suits that put the heavyset women to shame, as well as many who dressed conservatively in suit and tie. (The stereotype begun with the movie *Best in Show* was only partially accurate.) And there were the judges, kept in secret rooms under lock and key, so that they couldn't fraternize with the competitors, many of whom they knew on a first-name basis anyway.

There were also, once in a while, liaisons, with handlers emerging the morning after from the bedroom of owners, shoes in hand, spotted by those busybodies who regularly trolled the halls looking for gossip. These were the news items that didn't get printed in the tame and quickly-cobbled-together news-letter that arrived each morning under your door, but they circulated, rampant, anyway. In years to come the newsletter would be replaced with an email version that listed winners and congratulations to all.

At that year's National in Marin, there was going to be com-petition in and out of the ring. On the second afternoon before the sunset, there was a softball game that nearly everyone par-ticipated in. I hated softball because I was inept at it during high school, but I donned my required black-spotted jersey with feigned enthusiasm because I was trying to meet people and fit in. (All this social activity gave me anxiety and made me cling obsessively to Dawn, who knew absolutely everyone and flitted from group to group, with me hanging on her elbow.) At our game, where I struck out four times, the blacks vigorously op-posed the livers, wearing black and brown respectively, with the reward for the winning teams of T-shirts emblazoned with the name of the National's sponsoring club and the year.

Then there was the closing banquet, which was a dressy event, at least as far as the ladies were concerned—a chance to step things up a bit—though many of the guys still arrived in blue jeans and cowboy boots and some even with their Stetsons. The point was that everyone brought some flavor from his or her hometown and so made the mix a bit raucous. This par-ticular year, some inebriated member pitched a cherry tomato at someone at a nearby table who was equally gone, and it took only a minute for a food fight worthy of *Animal House* to begin, despite the beaded tops and suits. There was always someone with a childlike sense of fun that carried on despite the glares of those older and less flexible in their manners.

• • •

The last day of the National came, and along with it my class in the obedience ring, Novice B. I was waiting at the entrance, my number attached to my left arm with a rubber band. I checked my pockets again for the liver bait I used to entice Rhiannon to perform, as it was an instant disqualification to bring it into the obedience show ring. She sat patiently by my side. I was overwhelmingly anxious, but she seemed as relaxed as a cat in the sun. My number was called, and we entered. The heeling went smoothly, the down stay was a dream. Everything she did seemed perfect to me. We ended with a score of 195.5, in second place to a dog that was famous across the country for his brilliant obedience performances. I couldn't have been more delighted. For the first time I considered that maybe we had a chance for a Dog World Award, which were given to dogs competing in obedience who received their three "legs" with no score under 195. Suddenly anything with this incredible dog seemed possible. I was coming to love her more and more as we worked together. I was as bonded to her as she was to me.

The first day of our club's Specialty, following the National, brought Rhiannon and me one more challenge in the ring: her second leg for her Companion Dog title. I was more confident this time around, and that confidence proved to be well-founded—even though the male dog lying right beside her on the down leapt up and started wildly humping her. Tolerating the attack, Rhiannon never broke her stay, and we ended in first place with a score of 197.5—the best of all the scores at the Specialty. Rhiannon and I had won High in Trial. And so a dream came to be.

PART III

literati dalmatians

{IN ORDER OF APPEARANCE}

Rhiannon

The Theatreworks Puppies

Ashley

. . . and eight more

eight

I CHOSE *LITERATI* AS my kennel name, and though most people on the show circuit thought it was a play on the word *litter*, in reality, it was a merge of the word *literary*, which referred to my career as an author, and the slang term *glitterati*, which referred to those glamorous movie stars glittering in the stratosphere of success and public adoration. Everything I wished I could be, and everything I wished one of my dogs would be.

When 1994 arrived, it seemed an opportune time to breed Rhiannon. Even though she had not achieved all we had hoped, she had many worthy qualities. Perhaps, at a later point in my involvement in the Dal world, I might have been concerned that Rhiannon was not a good candidate for breeding because she had not yet finished her championship. However, Marty encouraged me to go ahead, and so—as we were still on the co-own contract—I sent Rhiannon on an airplane to Minnesota to a well-known stud, "Rob," who had sired many litters of champions. I was hoping that we would have some very pretty babies, and maybe even some livers, the more rare variety of Dalmatian that is brown-and-white spotted, rather than usual black-and-white. For the week before her time was due, I slept with her in Gabe's bedroom. He had been moved to Nathaniel's top bunk until the puppies were weaned at about four weeks old, when they would be moved into the garage.

I was alone in the house when she went into heavy labor. This wasn't like Penny's whelping when I was a young girl, sitting at the sidelines in horror at the show unfolding before me, accompanied by my parents. Here, I was an assistant to the ring mistress, and once again a bitch played the starring role. This time I could see with total amazement just how clearly she knew exactly what to do. The room echoed with grunts as she heaved and shoved and the first whelp appeared. She bent to tear open the sack, away from the pup's face, and I put my hands into the box to help her. She tolerated my presence easily. It was time to take care of the umbilical cord and I waited for her to begin to gnaw on it, but another pup was coming, fast now, and she didn't have a chance. I took over the first, trying to tie off the cord with the recommended dental floss, as my whelping book had suggested, but my hands shook and I couldn't manage it. I was overwhelmed with a sickening swirl in my head, and I thought I would throw up.

Scared, I lay down on the floor. After a minute, my head clear once again, I sat up and helped Rhiannon with the second pup. As I cleared the head out of the sac, she returned to the first and gnawed on the umbilical cord, saving me a second try with the dental floss. And from then on it was teamwork, her delivering, gnawing the cord, and starting to stimulate the pup with her tongue, me at last taking the puppy and rubbing it down briskly until it moved from dusky blue to pink and began to cry. Then I set it on her nipple to suckle until the next whelp arrived.

The fifth puppy slid out neatly, but Rhiannon nudged it only for a moment with her nose and then turned aside. I didn't understand at first, but when I grabbed it, I could feel how limp it was inside the sac. I tore the membrane away from the puppy's face and began rubbing with the towel, hard. The puppy didn't move. I suctioned its throat with a baby-sized bulb syringe and then did the "puppy shakedown," a well-known maneuver to breeders and vets, used when a puppy doesn't first respond. The pup is held up above the head and then swung down to the bottom of your chest, head supported, in an effort to clear the lungs of mucus and whelping fluids. I tried over and over, but the pup did not pink up. After twenty minutes of swinging and mouth-to-mouth resuscitation and rubdowns with towels, I laid the pup down, and Rhiannon gave me a knowing look. Into a garbage bag went the little body.

But six, seven, eight all arrived in fine shape. By the time the afternoon was over and the kids had peeked in the door, I had taken care of cleaning her bed and her body, and Rhiannon was settled on her side, nursing her pups. Nathaniel and Gabe came into the room softly and knelt at the side of the whelping box. I remembered my own morning so long ago with Penny and her litter: my disgust at what now seemed a natural process (perhaps because I had had my own children), and the love that came when my father put the first tiny puppy into my arms. That had been the first in a series of whelpings that never failed to amaze me. This was the second, and I was no less moved. Love came to me in two different ways: for Rhiannon and her travail, and for the helpless pups so dependent on her.

The boys were speechless at the sight of the pure-white piglets attached to Rhiannon's side, each decorated with a colored rickrack around the neck so that we could tell them apart. Slowly the boys reached out to touch them as I guarded Rhiannon's head to make sure she wouldn't snap as they neared a pup—but she only wagged her tail.

Over the next eight weeks, the pups grew and grew. At the end of week two they got their spots, and soon their eyes opened. Between weeks three and four they could certainly hear, or at least we thought they could, as this would not be certain until they had the BAER (brain auditory evoked response) test, which would tell us definitively whether they could hear in both ears, one ear, or none. A unilateral would be fine to place in a pet home, but any puppy totally deaf would have to be euthanized, a process I worried about, not only for myself, but especially for my boys. What would it teach them about the disabled: do we put them to sleep? Nevertheless, it was an ethical guideline I had agreed to when I joined the Dalmatian Club of America. Luckily, I did not have to face such a decision with this litter, because all checked out to be bilateral at the time of the BAER test.

At four weeks, the pups moved from the box in the house to the pen in the garage and stood on their sturdy hind legs to protest being confined. Their cries were persistent and piercing. The boys loved going out after school, sitting in the pen and letting the pups crawl all over them. We took picture after picture, and I worried about whom we would get to buy them. Or even give them away to. Just as my parents had Penny's pups.

But I needn't have worried. In the puppies' sixth week, the Golden Gate Kennel Club sponsored the biggest dog show of the West Coast, to be held, as always, at the Cow Palace in

South San Francisco. It was a "benched show," like Westminster, and required that all entrants remain on a long backless seat where you had twenty-four inches for each dog to lie on a bed or in a crate and be admired by the public. While those who passed by and ogled the dogs certainly had fun, it was hell for breeders and dogs, with people poking their hands and faces into the dogs' spaces, with those of us showing our dogs crammed onto the bench because there was nowhere else to sit, with the huge enclosed cow barns unheated. At that time it was a bitch of a show, but one you entered in order to be competitive. The Dalmatian Club of Northern California took up one entire fifty-foot bench.

I had entered Rhiannon three months earlier, before the autumn deadline, even though I had hoped she would be pregnant by then. Now, though I wouldn't show her, I could use my place on the bench to advertise the puppies. I took my best photos of them, made a glossy collage on a piece of eighteen-by-twenty-four–inch poster board, and put that in the space where Rhiannon was supposed to sit. By the end of the day I had seven deposits, all from puppy buyers, to the annoyance of other breeders on the bench who hadn't thought of such a trick and who were trying to sell their puppies by handing out their business cards. My method was such a resounding success that in future years, they prohibited the display of any kind of photos advertising your dogs on the bench because they felt it unfair. Jim brought the kids to the show, and I relinquished my seat happily so Nathaniel and Gabe could sit on the bench for a while, each grinning proudly

The puppies grew. I invited other breeders to help me evaluate the puppies, stacking them up on the grooming table and taking pictures, and then I decided which were show puppies and which were not. I chose the black-and-white girl with the yellow rickrack and Marty chose the liver girl to place with someone else in a co-own. All I knew was that I was glad that person wasn't me. I entertained prospective buyers like royalty, serving coffee and displaying the offspring, Rhiannon, and the pedigree. All homes were carefully screened and put through rigorous scrutiny before I would place a puppy.

However, to keep one of the puppies for myself was out of the question. I couldn't have another dog in the house. We already had Rhiannon and Tia, and Jim called a halt to raising a kingdom of dogs, even though I wanted to have the yellow puppy join the household. I needed to find a show home, just what I had originally been for Marty and Stu, where the new owners would allow me to co-own and show the puppy.

And find them I did—Pat and John Maciejewski. Pat had been in show business for a while, supervising her daughter's bid for professional song and dance. She and John were keenly interested in getting involved in another kind of show world. I told them there were no guarantees; the pup could turn out to be too colorful, or to have a lousy tail set and never do a thing in the breed ring. But I had a good feeling about this one, even though I was still a novice. She was beautiful, with ears marked in perfect symmetry, a dot right in the middle of each and just rimmed with black. Her top line was solid, her feet tight, and Rob had overcome Rhiannon's propensity for too much color. The Maciejewskis bought her and named her Literati's Show Biz Wiz, or "Ashley." She made a beautiful pair with their German shorthaired pointer, Max, with whom John liked to go pheasant hunting.

I did begin showing her, and she did begin winning. She held herself like a queen, upright and proud, with presence.

My instinct had been correct. The success made me feel as if I had finally grown up within the breed. People sometimes recognized me for my kennel name and my face and spoke to me with respect. The hobby had turned into something more, and I had learned that persistence pays off.

The Maciejewskis and I traveled all around the North and Southwest, sometimes with Dawn and sometimes without, showing Ashley to great success. Eventually Pat and John bought a huge, beautiful RV so that they could have a home away from home and became known for arriving at the show grounds with a loud honk on their horn, something the "Dalmatian Police" decreed obnoxious. Later, Ashley, Max, and the two puppies they kept from Ashley's first litter, Butler and Seren, would sleep up on the wide and deep dashboard, baking in the sunny warmth, despite my fears of a car crash. When Dawn traveled with us, we were once again sleeping in the same bed—this time the small and cramped pullout couch in the RV's living area.

Eventually, the Maciejewskis, totally smitten with the show world, asked if they could try their hand in the ring. Of course, I said yes, wanting them to experience what I had, and having less and less time to travel away from the family because of my growing sons and my writing. Pat and John loved the show circuit and eventually decided to have their own kennel name, taken from Ashley's moniker, Show Biz.

Jim had a new job, and increasingly it took him away from home. When Ashley completed her championship in 1996, a feat I had never been able to pull off with Rhiannon, I got many calls from those who wanted to congratulate me on my first homebred champion. Eventually Pat and John would put the handler Andy Linton on her, a professional now often seen winning at Westminster, and they began to "special" her. Taking her from one championship ring to another, we sought the coveted Best-of-Breed and Group wins and did receive a fair number of them. We persevered for a while, but winning had apparently given Ashley too much confidence and she began to get cocky, holding her tail up over her back too high, and thus she became less competitive. We retired her with regret—learning that even a terrific dog can change—and decided to breed her. It was time for another litter for Literati.

nine

IN JUNE OF 1997, we paired Ashley up with Dawn Mauel's very successful Group winner, Davenport. Ironically, Davenport was a son of Jack, Ashley's former nemesis in the ring. Pat and John and I arranged to co-own the litter. This time, however, I was there for the breeding, holding Ashley's muzzle even as she protested his entry.

Just as we had with Rhiannon's pregnancy, Jim and I, and John and Pat, were anxious to see whether she was pregnant— as my parents had been with Penny, though for an entirely different reason. Sure enough, it turned out she was in whelp. John and Pat didn't feel comfortable delivering a litter, so when her time came, I arrived on the scene better prepared than I had been with Rhiannon, feeling confident.

And it all went off easily. Mostly. Except for the fact that Ashley didn't want to stay in the whelping box and kept disappearing under the bed until I dragged her out so that she didn't deliver in a dark place where I couldn't see what was going on. Apart from some moderate amount of other assistance, Ashley did most of the work, just as her mother had. There, however, all resemblance to Super-Mom Rhiannon ceased.

Ashley was a terrible mother. Day after day, she deserted the whelping box to stand and howl at the baby gate that had been installed at the doorway to the room to keep her from escaping. She dug up the wall-to-wall carpeting in front of the door when she was left alone with the puppies. I credited all this to the fact that she'd been outrageously spoiled by Pat and John and was just trying to get out of the guest bedroom to be with everyone downstairs, rather than attending to her new family.

But at least she was willing to nurse them. They grew and grew and were the prettiest babies I'd yet had. They tromped on their rickrack and wrestled with each other, and I was delighted to see many of them had open markings when their spots came in. I didn't spend as much time with them as I had with Rhiannon's. I leaned on Pat for the day-to-day cleaning and handling, and she was good at it. I felt totally relaxed and didn't worry about how we would sell them.

The litter was growing up fast. The girl with the purple rickrack seemed a little off to me. Sometimes she growled when you held her, or sometimes she shied away and trembled with fear. Due to this sort of odd behavior, I began to suspect that she was deaf, even though I'd never had any experience before with a deaf puppy. At seven weeks, the BAER test confirmed that she couldn't hear in either ear, and I knew I faced the terrible decision. Pat, despite having agreed to the DCA ethical guidelines, greeted any suggestion of euthanasia with tears. Once again, I saw how breeding could be cruel, in imitation of the ways in which life was cruel. The day we took the puppy to the vet's office, Pat went with John and me, but she refused to come into the building. She paced the parking lot, smoking, and when we emerged, both John and me in tears, she fainted. We scooped her up off the blacktop and put her into the car. It took her a long time to recover.

It would be over twenty years before I would reconsider that decision to put an innocent pup to sleep, and decide—as a personal choice, for myself alone—that I would never do it again, providing the puppy had a sound temperament and could be placed in an appropriate home. But it is only recently that the argument over whether to put a "deafie" to sleep has begun to reverberate within DCA, and only now do some breeders admit that they are divided over what to do when a BAER test turns up a "flat line" in both ears.

We had no trouble selling the rest—partially because we kept so many of them. Despite the common wisdom that two pups would bond onto each other rather than onto their new families, Pat and John chose *both* a liver boy and a liver girl. The male pup with the green rickrack had caught my eye increasingly, and at last I convinced Jim to let me keep a third dog. This pup was handsome, with open markings and very black ears, and he liked to cuddle in my lap. I found myself handling him a lot, perhaps more than the other pups, and grew attached to him early on.

I stacked him up on the counter to look at his structure. I examined every spot on his body, having become what is known in the breed as "a spot counter," and I asked Dawn, in a ridiculous fashion, to help me determine how large those spots would spread. I was determined not to have too colorful a dog ever again, and it was obvious that from the amount of bone in his forelegs and the size of his paws that he would be big—but I liked big males. He had his mother's beautiful head shape, though one ear had a lot more spots than the other, which I knew would create a certain unevenness when it filled. I didn't really care. He stood up square and proud on Pat's countertop when we stacked him, and I knew that I would be taking him home.

I could not know it then, but his name would be Gulliver, and he was about to become the most important dog in my life.

· · ·

PART IV

dog of my heart

{IN ORDER OF APPEARANCE}

*Literati's Show Biz Mister Swift,
a.k.a. Gulliver*

ten

WE HAD TO GIVE him a literary name, of course. Ultimately, it was Jim who came up with Gulliver's show name, because he knew he would be nomadic, moving around the country to dog shows: Literati's Show Biz Mister Swift, after Jonathan Swift, who wrote *Gulliver's Travels*. It took a little while for "Gulliver," his call name, to grow on me. There would be many nicknames to come: Gully, Gullster, Baby Dog Baby Dog, Gullstiver, Gullsterama, Gulldog, Gullmeister, Mister, Dogoletto, Snoops—and a host of others I can no longer remember. Each endearment took firm hold and then after a while was inevitably less and less used as a new name was added, or it worked in new combination with those that followed. All of them meant "I love you."

For the first time, I was really running the show, although because I did co-breed the litter with the Maciejewskis, their kennel name, Show Biz, had to be part of the mix as well, but they followed my lead on every other decision.

Gulliver was the first dog we had who began to speak, and he did it a lot of the time. In full sentences, with real words. Through our mouths. Maybe this was one reason he had such a good sense of humor. His voice was like a little boy's, and it never got deep, even as he grew up and went through adolescence. He had a merry face with expressive brown eyes, one ear blacker than the other, and a beautifully shaped head.

On hot summer days, the pool in the backyard should have been a lure as powerful as the tree sticks he loved to gnaw on—even though he cracked a few back teeth. At least, that was what we heard from numerous friends whose goldens were clogging up their pool filters with thick fur. So on a warm day while Gulliver was still only a few months old, we dropped him into the shallow end to ensure that he knew how to get out at the broad circle of steps there—a ritual that all the dogs who came to live with us had to endure.

The pool was warm that first day, but this didn't seem to matter to Gulliver. Churning through the water, he looked for all the world as if he were drowning; with both his front and rear legs flailing away, he held his body in an upright position, his head barely above the small wake he was creating. He didn't skim the water with his snout flat and all four legs pumping below the surface like a Lab would have done. His eyes were panicked. I had to step down in my shorts and haul him out by the collar, even though by that point he was within reach of the stairway. After that, he refused, quite adamantly, to learn how to swim.

He would use the pool for only one thing: sitting on the wide top step to cool his bottom off in any kind of summer heat. Often he would sit that way for quite some time, looking around peaceably while all of us bent over with laughter.

Like any Dalmatian, he was always hungry and became a terrible thief. Anything within reach was fair game for counter cruising, and because of his height, everything was. When he went to stay with Dawn on some of our vacations, her kids nicknamed him "Pony Boy" because he could actually rest his chin, flat, on the top of their kitchen table.

After several months of losing pots of mashed potatoes and bowls of fruit—and especially hamburger—I began to set him up to catch him in the act. Though common dog wisdom said you couldn't punish a dog for something unless you caught him in the middle of the naughty behavior because they wouldn't remember even five minutes later, I rejected that notion, thinking privately that they managed to remember "cookie" perfectly well.

And so, up on the counter went mousetraps smeared with peanut butter. With my old riding crop in hand, I hid in the adjacent living room. After a while, sure enough, *Bang!* I raced in to see the mousetrap on the floor, sprung shut and kicked aside. I made a good show yelling, "Bad dog!" and of hitting the counters with the leather crop—but he was not to be fooled into thinking that I was about to smack him with it.

Despite my irritation at the mission having been foiled, I couldn't help but laugh at the spectacle he created with his long tongue licking in and out, his mouth nearly stuck shut with peanut butter, in a desperate attempt to dislodge the thick patch of goo sticking to the roof of his mouth. I gave up and learned to keep food at the back of the counters.

But this didn't keep him from the garbage cans: cleverly he balanced on his hind legs, tipping over the garbage—though the lids were fastened tight, or so I thought—to raid them for forbidden chicken bones or to spread clumps of used Kleenex all over the yard.

Any patch of sun was his to conquer, unlike the water in the pool—be it atop the big chair in the family room, or on the tile of the bathroom floor—or, most predictably, in our bed, especially when it wasn't made, so that he could snuggle his dirty paws and little white hairs down deep under the quilt. Often he could be found asleep in the white chaise lounge farthest from the pool, or even happily ensconced on his own in the hammock with a pillow. After that, the hammock became known as "Gulliver's swing."

He was growing into his big paws and would turn out to be sizeable. I liked that, because though he topped out at the standard's limit of nearly twenty-four inches at the withers, he looked substantial—and at that time, it was the fashion to have dogs small enough to look more like big bitches. Personally, I liked a dog to have size.

Gulliver's markings held true to what I'd seen when he first got his spots: he was reasonably open, with only a few secondaries, and his ears were coal black. His eyes were a good deep brown, though not as dark as some I'd seen, but I didn't really care. His structure was very good, and I had high hopes for him.

I held him out of the show ring until later the next spring, May of 1998—the National. I was nervous about starting out at the top, but I thought him exceedingly handsome, and so it seemed that a bit of a splash (no pun intended) was in order. The show was held in Kentucky that year, and Dawn and I flew out together, piling our suitcases and crates onto the plane, and once again sharing a room and a car rental.

As I dressed carefully that morning, trading off in the bathroom with Dawn for our showers, and then crowding in to put on our makeup in tandem, my nerves were getting the better of me. I slid into my suit, combed my hair, and gave Gulliver a final once-over. He was soft and clean, as I'd bathed and brushed him thoroughly before we left home, even though

Dals require little care in that regard. Still, brushing was a calming therapy for nerves. He loved it and always leaned into the rubber curry. If he could have purred, he would have. It appeared that he wasn't nervous at all.

As Gulliver and I flew around the ring that day, anxiety continued to course through me. I never lost the nerves, no matter how many times I showed. Part of me just believed that I would never have a top-winning dog. Ashley was the closest I had come, and even then, John and Pat had put a handler on her.

Gulliver and I were the last in line in all our classes that day, just by luck of the draw—but I was superstitious. I didn't think being at the back of the class, where the judge had to go over your dog after all the others, was such a great place to be. I liked being at the head of the line. First impressions count, I'd discovered, and sometimes, when a judge was confused by a big draw, he or she might just pick the first because it was easier. At least, this was what I, and some others I knew, believed.

As we flew past on the last go-round, me trying to keep up with this adolescent who could trot so fluidly, with plenty of reach in the front and lots of drive in the rear, I saw the judge pivot, and then point. At us! Gulliver gave me a two-legged hug when I bent to pat him in triumph and love. And then I gave a little jump, a caper that became known among my friends as the "Linda dance." I did it every time I won, out of sheer joy. As Gulliver hopped around while I hopped up and down, I realized something important: he loved the ring, and that quality was as important in a show dog as was sound structure or a pleasing spotting pattern. Attitude played an enormous role in how the dog appeared to the judge.

Gulliver won all three of his classes at the National: Futurity and Sweepstakes, as well as his regular puppy class. And a long-timer in the show world told me that it had been a long time since this had happened. Usually you were lucky to win one—it was rare to land all three. That night, Gulliver was able to continue Marty's tradition of a dog show hamburger after a win. I actually gave him three—one for each class.

As we took a photo with the judge to document the win so that I could run an ad in a dog magazine later, I had trouble stacking Gulliver. He kept moving his feet around, and I was getting frustrated. So were the photographer and the judge, who was well-known nationally and of whom I was a little bit intimidated. The judge always was included in the photo from a win, and I knew they had other photos to appear in and didn't like to be delayed by inept owners. I bit my lip and tried again.

"Move his left front foot forward," the photographer instructed, peering through his lens.

I did so, resetting it with care.

"No," he said testily. "The *left* foot."

Once again, I reset the foot. And the photographer sank back on his heels and sighed. It still wasn't right, though I couldn't have told you why.

"No, the *other* left foot," said the judge with a smile, and everyone began to laugh. Only then did I realize that I had been moving the right front foot back and forth. At last, I took up the left and moved it forward, there was a flash from the camera, and he clapped me on the back as we all left the ring, regaling Dawn and me with a bad joke that we promptly forgot.

Throughout the ensuing months, Gulliver's show career was a joy that penetrated the darkness of deepening personal problems at home: the beginnings of marriage trouble, the difficulties of parenting adolescent children, and the renewal of my long battle with depression. Yet, I often traveled with Pat and John in the RV, and Gulliver soon loved curling up in the sun with the other three dogs on the dashboard of the bus, as John motored down the long stretches of highway. The rest of us listened to Stephen King, Tom Wolfe, and John Irving on Books on Tape. Nights, John barbecued filets wrapped in bacon on the grill and Pat made pasta salads and invited everyone they knew—and increasingly they knew more people, as they traveled the circuits frequently in those days with Max, Ashley, Butler, Seren, and now Gulliver. Daytimes we entered classes and were gratified to find our dogs winning. What a wonderful distraction it was from the parts of my life I didn't want to look at.

eleven

SOMETIME BEFORE I WENT off on the show circuit with
Gulliver, many aspects of my home life started to go awry.
Just prior to Ashley's whelping and Gulliver's birth, Rhiannon
and Tia had begun to fight intermittently. It began in 1998,
with a disagreement over a bagel that Nathaniel was waving
enticingly over their heads, which quickly developed into a
squabble. No one could tell me which dog had started it. A
week later, there was a more-lengthy contretemps with teeth
bared: it began with a warning growl, then a snap, and then an
explosion of noise that made both me and Gabe first draw back
and then plunge in, quelling it within seconds by pulling the
two dogs apart. It had sounded fierce but in the end drew no
blood, and thus seemed minor to me at that point, a disagreement between two dogs who had simply grown momentarily
weary of one another. The episode was not repeated, and six
months went by, quietly.

And then, suddenly, for no apparent reason I could discern,
the dogs were at war. First it was quarreling, and then, with an
explosion, it was full-blown fighting. It could be over something as simple as a toy, but then it was over nothing any of us

could perceive—perhaps just a glance, even, that only a dog would interpret as a challenge. But Tia was growing, an adolescent now. Rhiannon, not an aggressive dog, had grown possessive of me and of her place as the head of the pack, and Tia was threatening that dominant position.

Having added a new puppy to the mix probably didn't help, as he, too, drew my attention away from Rhiannon. As the fights developed into more and more confrontations, I grew alarmed, even more so when Gabe was traumatized and frightened by one that happened right at his knees. Increasingly, the fights ended with trips to the vet to stitch up both dogs.

I was at a loss. I'd had no experience with aggression or how to read the signs of an imminent altercation. All my dogs, back into my childhood, had always prospered together and been glad for one another's company. All the dog fights I'd ever seen had been between dogs who were strangers, as when my Aunt Joan's Boston terrier, Jingo, had come home covered in bloody welts after a run-in with the neighbor's poodle. And so we entered a period of time during which I was on constant alert, filled with anxiety that something would set Rhiannon and Tia off again into another event from which the family would have difficulty recovering. Where dogs had always served as a comfort for me in the years of my childhood, now they were the source of anxiety. Now I could not trust them the way I had trusted Daisy, Penny, Gidget, and Clover, and this was a loss.

I decided that everyone would be safer if they were crated in separate rooms and were let out only individually until a solution could be found, but I knew that safeguards like these were imperfect at best. There was too much that could go wrong, too many ways that a mistake could be made.

At this point, I resorted to consulting a "dog psychic," something that would have seemed humorous if I hadn't been so desperate. I needed to understand better: hoping for insight into why Rhi and Ti were fighting and what I could do to solve it, I nevertheless kept this move a secret from everyone except Jim and the kids, and Kathryn, Pat, and Dawn. It felt perfectly reasonable to me, considering the dire nature of our situation; sometimes you needed to take extraordinary measures when it came to solving the extraordinary problems of your dogs. I wouldn't have hesitated to take my kids to a psychiatrist, so why did taking the dogs to a psychic seem so strange? The two dogs and I huddled together around the phone, as their proximity was apparently required, and despite a healthy dose of skepticism, I somehow wasn't at all surprised that she seemed to know a great deal about my dogs and their emotions. I found myself accepting all her advice easily.

One day, Pat and I went to a local show, and as I took both Tia and Rhiannon out of their car crates while keeping careful distance between them, I stumbled and went down. With a growl, the two were off and fighting. Pat, restraining Ashley at the same time, reached down to try and separate them. As she put her hand into the mix, one of them snapped, hard, and her finger was caught in the vicious tangle. The bite broke no skin, but she was in pain nevertheless.

It was clear to me now that something new had to be done with the two dogs. In desperation, I finally called a behaviorist in canine aggression recommended by one of the members from DCNC. Julia Barrows dug deeply into her bag of tricks. We tried all sorts of things to establish each dog's submission to me, emphasizing that I was the alpha dog directing the household, not either one of them.

At first, many of the exercises did work. We tied black trash bags of shaker cans (soda cans filled with pennies) to the knobs of every door in the house, in case an altercation developed. The bags did help, as they made a tremendous racket that the dogs found unnerving, but despite this, the intervals between the fights were shortening—even though with people, both Rhiannon and Tia continued to be exceedingly gentle and friendly. Neither of them ever raised a hackle to a human. This conundrum led me to the conclusion that they could, with time, be rehabilitated. Julia agreed.

However, nothing seemed to have an effect for very long. After a while, over my fears and strong reservations, Julia convinced me to try shock collars. The collars delivered an electrical pulse preceded by a warning beep when you pushed a button in reaction to any onset of aggression, such as the mere vibration of a growl. I wanted to know exactly what my dog would feel, and so I strapped one of the transmitters on my upper arm. It was a shock indeed, but not a drastic one, and I convinced myself that it was a necessary step.

At first, it seemed to deter them, but ultimately it backfired, provoking them to attack, as each thought the other was sending the stinging jolt. It only made them angrier with each other, and I realized then that I needed to listen better to my own instincts. I insisted that we remove the collars, and we went back to straight behavioral modification. My hope was waning.

Gulliver had watched all the aggression from the sidelines and tended to hide beneath any nearby piece of furniture. I could see no obvious effect on him from the fighting. He still seemed a happy-go-lucky dog who got along with everyone in the house, including the two older dogs, and I fantasized that he would help resolve the situation.

But finally, after many more fights and thousands of dollars spent on the surgeries required to stitch Rhiannon and Tia back up, Julia and I came to the terrible decision that should another fight occur, I would have to put the dogs to sleep. In the meantime, I began, with panic, to try to find them new homes. But inside, I didn't really believe that they would have to go. And I started going over the possibilities in my mind.

Initially, I rationalized keeping Rhiannon, my close friend and obedience champ. But then I worried that she might feel threatened by Gulliver as he grew older, just the way she now felt threatened by Tia. And exuberant Tia—who knew if she could be reliable with other dogs? I began a campaign among other breeders I knew, looking for a different spot for each dog, but no one would take them. I did not dare look to place them in the world of pet owners. How could I give away a dog that was unpredictable with aggression, and who had fought so viciously? I could not guarantee safety with other dogs or, perhaps eventually, with other people.

And then, miraculously it seemed, the dogs calmed down and accepted each other once again. One day, they didn't seem so angry, and so after a week of watching them, I let them approach each other and sniff, on leash. Little by little, we all began to relax again. In the matter of a few weeks, they were sleeping together on their beds rather than in their crates, they ate from bowls side by side and drank water from the same dish. One day, I watched them run across the lawn, rising and falling in the natural rhythm of two dogs playing together as friends. Gulliver frisked along beside them. Happiness buoyed inside us all. And in this way, an entire year and a half passed, and the trauma of the past fights receded into an old memory.

However, one afternoon in October of 1997, without warning or provocation, the situation exploded once again. Rising in rage, the two girls went at each other with their teeth in a battle of renewed fury. This time it was nearly fatal, with terrible gashes in their snowy coats, deep puncture wounds on their heads and around their eyes. Tia locked onto Rhiannon's ear, and when I tried to pry it from her mouth, it tore down to the very edge, hanging on by only a single strip of skin. I wrapped her head in a towel, shoved them both into their crates in the minivan, and sped to the vet. I was angry and I was scared. At last I knew I couldn't save them. For the safety of others, these dogs, who had become so inexplicably aggressive, had to be put down.

I brought Tia in first. I knew it would be harder with Rhiannon. In an instant, Tia died in my arms. I cut off all my emotions and didn't allow myself to feel. I don't remember whether I cried, or how I stilled the clamor in my heart.

Then I struggled to lift Rhiannon and carry her in from the car. I refused the help of a vet tech. This was something I had to do on my own, from beginning to end. I sat down on the gray linoleum floor with her body drawn up close across my legs, put my arms around her, and cradled her head. Her ear was torn from her head, her pain obvious. The vet's needle pricked through her coat and then found the vein in her front leg. As I looked deeply into her eyes, they went blank and her face relaxed. My special dog was gone.

The vet asked me if I wanted the dogs' ashes after cremation. I was in a state of shock. Already I knew that I would never, ever, forgive myself. I shook my head and regretted the decision, always.

Jim came to pick me up. When we drove home together—abandoning my car in the parking lot temporarily—I couldn't even cry. I felt dry inside and exhausted. The feeling reminded me of something. At first I couldn't identify it. Then it came to me: the numbness I had felt at my mother's death. The day I had stumbled, unable to feel either curb or pavement, to the place I would learn of her suicide. And then, the day we had buried Daisy in the backyard. All the days of loss. Jim put me into bed and pulled up the covers to stop my body from shaking. I pulled the sheet over my head to shut out the light, but I could hear him scrubbing as he began to wash the blood from the fight off the wall.

Gulliver jumped up to curl beside me. I pulled the sheet back and held on to him as tightly as I thought a young pup could bear. Surprisingly, he lay beside me for a very long time, comforting me with the warmth of his body. It would not be the last time he was there as a solace, or helped me continue to go on breathing despite emotion coursing through me. Perhaps I was comforting him as well: over the ensuing days, his fear and loneliness at the disappearance of Rhiannon and Tia was palpable.

The loss of my two beloved dogs was not my only trouble. Shortly before Rhiannon and Tia did their final lethal dance, my mood had plummeted after the rejection of my latest novel by various New York publishers. The positive reviews for my previous work seemed far behind me—not forgotten exactly, but just belonging to another part of my life. After I put Rhiannon and Tia down, I fell into a deep depression, part of a newly diagnosed bipolar disorder. My marriage began to disintegrate in earnest, and I despaired of ever righting myself again.

The world grew black, and I couldn't shake my negative thoughts. My therapist diagnosed what I was going through as a clinical depression, which was far worse than the intermittent episodes I had experienced as a teenager and then as a new mother. That year was the twenty-fifth anniversary of my mother's suicide, which had occurred when she was forty-five; I was approaching my own forty-fifth birthday, and I could not face my writing room or my kitchen. I could not look the world in the eye, and sometimes I went back to bed in the morning after I had made breakfast for the kids and driven them to school. In December, I made a suicide attempt, an act that devastated the family and drove Jim even further away. The children were shaken, angry, frightened, certain that they were the ones who must somehow keep me alive, despite my protestations that this was not so. Before the depression ended some seven years later, I tried to kill myself three times; despite intermittent moments of relief, the undertow always sucked at my ankles and threatened to bring me down.

Determined to keep the burden of my desperation from descending on anyone else, in my despair, I began to depend on Gulliver. He was willing to lie beside me on the bed every day for the hours I fled from the world. When friends drew back, repelled by difficulties with my newly diagnosed disorder, when family grew angry with me and let me know exactly how they felt, when Jim finally left me for another woman—Gulliver was the one who was there for me. Though he never had the opportunity to visit a nursing home or make his way through the corridors of a hospital to comfort a sick stranger, he had nevertheless become a therapy dog—my therapy dog—a role Daisy had once played for my mother.

Many days I lay on my bed without getting dressed. I rose only to do things for the children. I had stopped working. My mood had slipped down into a dark, grim "rabbit hole," as I described it to my psychiatrist. The bedroom was my sanctuary, a place to feel safe, and Gulliver was the sentinel there. When I cried, he licked away the salt of my tears. Sometimes I would spend hours tracing the black spots that were scattered across the bridge of his nose, or beneath his eyes and his muzzle. For Gulliver, there was no such thing as too much bed. Or too much love. In either direction.

Some things would drive me up out of the sheets. Gulliver was my alarm clock for every deadline. 7:00 AM: Time to feed Gulliver and then rouse the boys for school. Noon: Time to let Gulliver out to potty, as he jumped from the bed and stood there staring at me expectantly by the bedroom door. 3:00 PM: Time to pick up the kids and drive them to after-school activities, as Gulliver now waited in the kitchen, ready to jump into the car, where he would then claw his way forward from the backseat, putting his paws onto the armrest of the driver's seat and craning his neck to stick his nose out my window because the van didn't have a second row that opened. 5:00 PM sharp: Once again time to feed Gulliver, who circled his food bowl with a variety of groans, and then time to start working on the kids' dinner, even if it was just basic chicken and rice. 6:00 PM: Check-in, as Gulliver roused himself from his postprandial nap; if time had gotten away from me, he followed me with determination until I stopped wandering through the house aimlessly instead of setting the table and supervising homework.

I tried to keep up appearances, not to let neighbors and friends know how truly desperate I was, but with Gulliver, I held nothing back. And he didn't mind. His eyes held sadness over my desolation, but he was not deterred by my need. True to his unspoken promise to stick around no matter what, he was there through each day, every day. Nothing about what I was enduring scared or disgusted him. He loved me without reservation, the way I wished my family would. He'd bump up against my legs, leaning his weight against me to reassure both of us, just the way a cat twines itself in and around your calves as a way of showing affection.

I needed his vigilance, as he used his warmth to anchor me to reality. He provided me the comfort a friend, a child, or even a partner could not. He had become my best friend—someone with whom I could commune. Someone who loved me, no matter how far I had fallen or how unattractive I had become, and someone whom I could love back, no matter how imperfect the love I offered. I never disappointed him, and he never disappointed me. He never remembered my faults. He never failed to dial in to my mood.

Unlike my teenagers, who were entrenched in their own adolescent battles, he never fought with me, never mouthed off, and never muttered, "Fuck you!" behind my back. Without realizing it, I was beginning to learn something new and important: the lively countenance of a dog reminds us we are human, yet at a remove from the fact that we are mortal. With Gulliver's help, I was very gradually beginning to rouse myself from my sheets and do more than just watch the stream of life beyond my bedroom window.

• • •

We turned the corner into spring, and I made a greater effort to conquer the depression. Despite my grief over losing Rhiannon and Tia, despite the continuing cycle of mania and depression and the aftermath of the first suicide attempt, and even despite Jim's absence, I picked up with Gulliver in the ring as the new show season began, with the encouragement of Pat and Dawn. I thought that perhaps getting back into showing Gulliver would help me get out of my own inner world, and so I entered him here and there whenever I could manage.

Showing was one of the only things that encouraged me to move from the psychological adhesive of my bedroom when the children were not around. Still, I made no attempt to start obedience training with him, as it was just too painful to remember how proficient Rhiannon had been.

My new psychiatric medications, designed to treat my bipolar disorder, proved to be a problem. Sleepiness often overwhelmed me, and to my embarrassment, I sometimes dozed off between classes as I waited for ours. Dawn and Pat couldn't figure out what was wrong with me and grew puzzled and perhaps annoyed.

Despite this, I showed Gulliver intermittently throughout the summer months, piggybacking the two of us onto Pat and John's attendance as a way of avoiding being by myself or of driving alone while sleepy from medication. But with time, the emotional trauma stemming from the previous aggression between Rhiannon and Tia began to create a problem for Gulliver. Though he had crawled under the big bed during that last fatal fight, he had nevertheless been a witness. And therefore a victim. When he hit adolescence, as we passed other dogs as we walked to and from show rings, he would growl, deep down in his throat, inaudibly—but I could feel the vibration come up the lead into my hand. He was frightened, I realized.

It was an autumn day in September, brilliantly clear and still warm, as California always is at that time of year. We entered the ring feeling confident: he had only another point to go to earn his championship. Stacked up before the judge, I thought he looked great, and I began to hope for the win.

But as we waited in line, another dog made his final circuit in front of the judge and then came up behind us full speed and crowded Gulliver against the ring rope. In defense (perhaps remembering another time, when his housemates had turned on each other), he swung around and lunged at the strange male. He was a big strong dog on a thin show lead, and I barely managed to keep hold of him. The other owner began to yell at me, and I told him it was his own fault for "running up" on us. Etiquette, and common sense, demands that you give the dog in front of you plenty of space. No one likes his territory to be encroached on, especially not show males who are already keyed up. The judge approached and asked the woman who preceded us in the line if she were having trouble with my dog. She answered no, quite honestly, and the man behind me subsided with a grumble. That ended the issue. But not for long.

Sunday, as Gulliver and I entered the ring for his class, I began to worry that—if it happened again—I wouldn't be able to control him. We were in the same order in line as the day before, the same dog behind us. I took a lot of freeze-dried liver from my pocket to distract him. It was his favorite bait and kept him occupied for a while.

I maintained a good distance between us and the pair behind. But I could feel Gulliver's tension begin to move up the lead. I kept distracting him as I stacked him. In spite of all this, everything went well. We finished the last go-round, and the judge made his decision. We weren't the ones he pointed to, but I didn't even feel let down. I was just grateful and relieved that there hadn't been another incident. While I was momentarily distracted by negotiating my way out of the ring amid all the other dogs, Gulliver lunged hard against the lead, and it tore through my hands, which were slippery from all the liver I had been handling. With an angry bound, he began to chase the dog who had crowded him the day before, right out of the ring.

Though I was close behind him, I couldn't keep up. As he ran, there were the usual shouts of "loose dog." Generally, someone caught the escapee, and that was the end of it, but this day, by the time I found him again, he had bitten the other dog on the haunches. Not a bad bite, but a bite nonetheless. I pulled him from the following show the next day.

After waiting for a while, and then, on the basis of advice from several of my friends in the breed, I reluctantly decided that our career in the show ring was over, even though he needed only that single point to finish his championship. At home, I at last sunk into the mire of an even darker time. Never again would I be in the ring beside him. It was over.

• • •

Pat and Dawn were supportive and stood by me faithfully during this time, but they didn't really understand what I was going through. On the other hand, Myrna Robinson did, a woman I had met nearly as soon as I arrived in California. She was a therapist with a master's degree in social work, who had divorced in nearly the same year Jim had moved out. She was extremely petite and finely boned, with deeply set dark brown eyes that almost always held a gentle expression. We both served on the boards of two charitable organizations and, as divorced women, had the same amount of free time on our hands. Myrna understood, kept me afloat, came to visit me at the hospital every day. It was Myrna who initially drove me back and forth to my outpatient therapy after my second suicide attempt in the spring of the following year.

She invited me over for dinner, and lunch when she was not working, to go to a movie on a Saturday night, intuiting that it was important for me not to be alone. Though she knew nothing about dogs, Gulliver was always welcome, too, and she stored one of his special sheepskin blankets in her front hall closet, claiming not to care when the space beneath the coats became fragrant with an unmistakable musky odor. Loving Gulliver, it seemed, was another way of loving me.

Even though I had been terrible about returning her phone calls, Pat had been determined to reach me in spite of my depression. She hadn't tried to talk me into resuming the show circuit with Gulliver once I had pulled him for aggression, even though she and John went on to finish Seren's and Butler's championships and to take enormous pleasure in the achievement of doing it themselves rather than with a handler, driving their "bus" from state to state. I didn't try to explain to her what was going on with me on a personal level. She just intuited and accepted it.

Dawn, too, continued to try to reach out, but I'm not sure she really fathomed the bleak world I had entered. It frustrated her, perhaps, when I turned down her offers for shopping or lunch. Pat didn't seem to mind so much. She just wanted a chat on the phone, and sometimes a chat was all I could manage. Joy and Dad didn't call much, so I was reliant on friends instead of family.

. . .

I began to date occasionally, and I used Gulliver as the bellwether of the potential success of a new relationship. As the expected guy came up the front walk to our house, I would let Gulliver loose to greet him, allowing him to bark madly at the intrusion of the stranger. When Tom, Dick, or Harry came quickly to a halt and stood with his hands frozen against his thighs, I knew that they were not dog lovers, let alone dog people, and at the back of my mind was the thought that they had failed Gulliver's test, no matter how charming they might turn out to be. Their hearts, it would inevitably turn out, were not as warm and open as both Gulliver and I required.

One late afternoon, Brad Clink came to pick me up for our first date. As Gulliver took off and began to bark—his approach steady and fast as a fighter jet—Brad dropped to one knee and opened his arms, welcoming the speedy bullet of a dog straight into his chest. Gulliver flew in on target, all elbows and knees, and began to lick Brad's face with ecstasy. Brad returned each kiss with a nuzzle of his own, thumping Gulliver happily on the ribs, calling him "a good ole boy." He'd kissed my dog before he'd even kissed me.

Brad had been divorced for thirteen years, having been thrown into the role of single parent to two daughters when his alcoholic wife left him. His kids were just about the same age as mine, he was crazy about dogs, he loved the movies, and sailing, and the symphony, and all these things we had in common attracted me. After our fourth date, I took the initiative, and, trying not to sound too eager, I asked him out again, even though it had only been two days since we'd last seen each other.

He lived on the other side of the bay, nearly an hour's drive away, so we had to make a determined effort to get together. Little by little, we both stopped dating anyone else, and now at night I sat on my bed, and with my arm wrapped around Gulliver, talked with Brad on the phone. When we ran out of things to say, we just listened to each other breathe. I met his youngest daughter, and we got along right away, and my kids seemed to accept him, guardedly, as well, telling friends that their mom had a boyfriend. Both Dawn and Pat approved of Brad, and that helped me let him into my heart and into my home. Brad felt their affection and returned it.

After the initial two months of weekend movies and picnics in Stern Grove, where the symphony gave Sunday-afternoon concerts, he asked me to join him on a road trip to Florida, where his older daughter was stationed in the navy. She needed her car, and he had offered to drive it to her in Pensacola.

I agreed. Myrna was shocked: "You barely know him," she protested. "He could be an ax murderer!" Dawn and Pat laughed, and they thought I was equally nuts.

But I had never seen the Grand Canyon, or the Painted Desert, or the stretches of towns and cities we would travel through on our way to Florida. Even my psychiatrist thought I should take the risk. We had to leave Gulliver behind, but I hired a good babysitter for him, and Jim agreed to take the kids. I really didn't like the idea of leaving my dog (and neither did Brad), but the small two-seater car didn't have room for him, and it wasn't practical in any case. I would just have to have fun without him, for a short time.

And I did, my spirits lifted by something new as we motored through small towns and big cities, dining on grilled cheese sandwiches and chocolate milk shakes for both lunch and supper at one Denny's after another, and staying in cheap motels. The miles sped by, and the little Mazda's air conditioner broke down, so we traveled with the windows open, singing sixties tunes loudly over the hot wind. We passed through Albuquerque, spent several nights with Brad's relatives in Dallas and Houston, and then finally reached Memphis, where we floated down the Mississippi on a paddleboat and met up with Brad's daughter and her drill team, the Navy Crackerjacks, who were performing there. Afterward, we trailed their bus back down to Pensacola, where we spent time visiting with her and rolling around in the warm waters of the Gulf.

When we returned, Gulliver was of course ecstatic (naturally the boys were less so, having been thrilled with all the freedom while being at Jim's house). And I had learned that I could indeed survive—if only for a little while—without Gulliver.

· · ·

I wasn't so alone anymore. On the weekends when the kids were with Jim, Brad stayed overnight, in secret. My depression persisted but loosened its grip a bit. In addition to relying on Gulliver, I now could rely on Brad. Still, Gulliver didn't leave my side and insisted that if Brad wanted to be a part of the family, he would have to accept a dog's well-earned spot on the bed. Brad didn't mind at all. It had been many years since he had had a dog in his life, and he took Gully into his heart as fully as Gully took Brad into his. It looked as if we had added another stable person to our quartet.

Gulliver had a way of worming himself into your soul, not only with the honesty and integrity in his limitless gaze, which made him seem so human. But there were also the continuing antics as he aged, antics that belied the fact that he was no longer a youngster: after we bought a sailboat in 2000, he would bark furiously at Jet Skis—even though the enormous oil tankers and container ships, which rose up a mile high beside us on the San Francisco Bay, didn't intimidate him at all; he persistently snuggled between Brad and me on the bed so that he could claim strokes from both sides; he was so determined to be near me that he squashed himself into the kink of my bent legs as I lay watching prime time.

In the morning, his cold nose roused me from sleep and nudged me upright, leaving me no choice but to go and feed him, urging me on as he sacked me behind my knees in a rugby tackle. After breakfast, he went eagerly to the back door, but then, if it was raining, he changed his mind and would refuse to go out, no matter how desperately he needed to pee. When I went up the driveway to get the newspaper, Gulliver rollicked beside me happily, with his ears flying in the wind, his body curving back and forth in a rocking horse motion reminiscent of a Lippizaner. Late in the afternoon, having been curled in the overstuffed and dilapidated armchair beside my computer as he put in a "hard day's work" alongside me, he would "smile" his special Dalmatian grin from where he turned to wait for me on the top step of the steep stairs down to my writing cottage.

Still, I often worried that something would happen to Gulliver. The loss of Tia and Rhiannon—so recent—continued to plague me. Nighttimes, trying to sleep, terrible pictures of what might happen to him if he got himself tangled up with a bigger, more vicious dog, or if we had an earthquake and he was trapped beneath the house, or if the boat tipped over on the bay and he was carried away by the currents—all sorts of ridiculous scenarios invaded my mind to torture me. I would roll over and will myself to sleep. The fact was that I could not imagine my life without him.

twelve

SLOWLY, AS THE YEARS of the new century began to pass, life once again came to seem more precious. Little by little, I started to shake off my dark moods. Occasional work on what would turn out to be a new memoir, long therapy sessions, continual monitoring of my medication, and the love of Brad and Gulliver began to pull me back from the edge. My children still stood beside me. However, my sister remained wary—slower to warm up—not trusting me to make the changes permanent, and not willing to commit herself to love again until I was truly well. My struggles reminded her of my mother's illness, and she confused the two without even realizing it. And my father was still crippled by worry, an attitude that felt like a reproach to me.

Brad and I had moved out of the house that Jim and I had bought back in 1989, when we first moved to California. It was filled with memories of my marriage, of my life as a young mother with our family, and I felt I couldn't move on again until I was in a new place, making a new beginning. We found a much smaller home with beautiful views of the rolling and deeply forested mountains from every window, mountains that were undisturbed by any houses high up on their peaks.

Myrna, who was an interior designer in her free time, helped us to sort through the oversize furniture that was too big, and to find new chairs and tables that would fit.

Nathaniel and Gabe had gone off to college, so Gully was the only one accompanying us to our new home, where he resumed his usual spot by my side, using up all the space on the bed. He hugged closer to me, even though my shrink questioned the wisdom of allowing a dog to sleep between us. He loved Brad in a way he hadn't loved Jim, perhaps because Jim had not loved him back in quite that manner.

• • •

We built a fence around the property, hating to interfere with our spectacular views of the mountains around us, but needing to keep Gulliver in as he displayed a new propensity to wander. The fence, however, did not stop him from digging under the chain-link and escaping out into the canyon below. When I went out onto the deck to discover where he had gotten himself to, Gulliver always looked up from munching on a fat patch of grass with a look of contentment and smugness. Fortunately, he never went very far and would always come back as I called him with the sound of a metal rod on a triangle, just the way I had watched the cook call the ranch hands for supper on the television show *Bonanza*. Gulliver would bound up the slope and was always rewarded either with his food pan or a cookie.

In time, we gave up on the chain-link and put up an "invisible" fence, which ran a wire around the yard to keep him from trespassing across the boundaries either by digging under or flying over. Gulliver wore a collar with a little box on it, one that made two loud warning tones and then administered a buzz against the throat (once again, I strapped the collar on my arm to determine how much of a jolt it actually delivered, and finally approved the level at which it was set). With just one buzz, Gulliver learned not to venture farther than the line marked with red flags and shortly became an expert at determining where the warning tone would sound. If I went up the steeply winding driveway to get the mail from the box on the road, he paced back and forth between the two flags. He'd whine, anxious for me to come back down, but never once breaking across the invisible barrier.

Now I had a full-fledged writing cottage instead of a room in the house, a little gray-shingled studio down the steep hill that led to the bottom of the property. We revamped it with an inexpensive built-in desk and bookshelves, and Myrna approved my choice of a warm yellow paint for the walls. I had shaken off the blanket of depression enough to begin clacking away on my computer, writing just a bit every other day or so, in my mind calling it a journal, rather than a book. I kept rewriting, revising material tirelessly as a way of keeping my sense of creativity alive, even when I was too blue to do anything new. Gulliver curled up in the worn armchair I had set in the sun by the double French doors.

I despaired that I would ever go back to writing full-time. Sometimes I commented to Brad that I wasn't getting any work done, and he would say, "Your only job is to get well." And with that he would clap his hands, and Gulliver would jump up to curl at my feet on the couch, to which I had moved after graduating from sleeping on the bed all day. I was learning, hour by hour, how love could build a net beneath you to keep you from falling, as both Brad and Gulliver helped me see. Gulliver never surrendered his role as caretaker, but he especially seemed genuinely happy when I began coming to my feet once again. As I grew older and better, he relaxed into middle age.

• • •

One of the things we did as I got better was buy a sailboat. It wasn't huge, but it wasn't small, either, and we could sleep comfortably on its queen-size bed. Gulliver slept on the couch in the salon, even though every night he tried to weasel his way onto the bed, but he was just too big not to crowd us, so we always kicked him off. I didn't allow myself to feel sorry for him: he did have a thick rug on which to curl up. Gradually, sailing every weekend replaced what dog shows had meant in my life. It was something Brad and I shared, and so my love of it grew with my love of him.

To our surprise, Gulliver enjoyed being out on the water as much as we did. Despite his tethering chain, he would hunker down on one of the cushions in the cockpit, up under the windscreen, and put his chin down on the pile of coats that were heaped up there, ready for the cold winds of San Francisco Bay that blew year-round. Within seconds, he would be oblivious, with his big paws curled beneath his chin. He did sleep a lot on the boat, and at home, and Brad said he wanted a dog's life: just sleeping, eating, and pooping.

After a long nap, Gulliver would put his head out into the breeze, and his ears flew back even further than they did when riding in the car, but I suspected that it was the same sensation that drew him to do it. He would attentively sit and watch the huge cargo ships go by, or the other sailboats as they heeled over in the sharp wind. At lunchtime, he hunkered down on the sole of the boat, waiting for a bite of sandwich to fall. My tuna, thick with mayonnaise, was his favorite.

While Gulliver was happy to watch the trawlers and the tugboats and the huge cargo containers, he drew the line at the smaller motorboats, Jet Skis, and parasailers. As they passed us with a hiss and unexpected speed, not looking like anything he'd ever seen before, he barked wildly and tried to climb out of the cockpit and attack them. I would always pull him back in and scold him, but for once he ignored me and just struggled against his tether, despite my admonitions.

Once a humpback whale breached right beside us, but even Gulliver was silent at the awesome sight as it spouted out through its blowhole, dove, came up to spout once more, and then disappeared forever. It was an experience neither Brad nor I would ever forget.

Our first weekend on the water together took us to China Camp, so called because of the Asian population who gravitated there in the early part of the century to make their livelihood harvesting shrimp. We lowered the dingy for the first time to take Gulliver ashore to potty. We got halfway to the sandy beach when the engine quit. We had oars, but Brad yelled at me to grab the emergency sail bag. I felt for it with both hands under the seat, but when I at last retrieved it, it was empty. In our amateur's enthusiasm, we had forgotten to bring with us either a cell phone or our handheld radio, or even the dinghy's small anchor.

The current began to move us farther and farther away from the boat, farther and farther away from shore. Gulliver huddled in the bow and made not a sound, seeming to sense what a dangerous situation we were in. Luckily, with Brad rowing all out, I was able to just catch the handhold on the stern of the boat as the dingy swirled toward the ocean. It was one of the most harrowing experiences we ever had on the boat.

"We'll never forget that stuff again," commented Brad in a shaky voice, as he wiped the sweat from his forehead.

That night, because the engine had failed, we were unable to take Gulliver to shore to potty. Many other sailors had dogs on their boats, especially the liveaboards, and all had advised us that we ought to teach him how to potty on the deck for those times when we were unable to get to shore, such as a dark, late night. Of course, we hadn't done that. We decided that we would give him a try before calling it a day and agreed that if he didn't potty onboard, we would pack up and go home.

The first night passed, with us entreating him, "Potty, potty," on the deck, my anxiety over the situation deepening. He had been well house-trained, and the deck was part of the boat and the boat was part of home, and so he refused to go. And on it went through the next morning and afternoon. By now I was really worried and couldn't even concentrate on enjoying myself. I convinced Brad, who was resolved to try to wait him out a little bit longer, that we would leave by five o'clock if he hadn't given in.

Then, as we were getting ready to pull the anchor, Gulliver neatly raised one leg and peed right over the side of the deck. He hadn't given in and soiled on the boat—but instead had figured out a way to relieve himself over the lifeline. Over the years, he never would poop onboard, preferring to hold it till our weekend jaunts either brought us to some shore or back to the slip. In later years, there was another sandy beach at Paradise Cove, which we dubbed "Gulliver's Beach," where we would often take him to pee and romp—largely because the China Camp beach seemed so difficult to land on with its swift currents. But whenever we tried China Camp, we made certain that the engine was always carefully primed and pretested.

Back at the slip, to get up onto the boat, he was meant, like a human, to carefully climb the three steps we had installed for people and dogs alike, so that you didn't have to hike yourself up so high or jump down so hard when getting on or off. Gulliver refused those steps, as if they were beneath his dignity, and would use only the very top step as a platform from which to leap onto the boat. This was fine when he was a young dog, but as he aged, he couldn't always make the deck. Several times he fell into the water and had to be rescued by me pulling him up by his collar with all my strength. Then he stood on the dock, shaking the salty water from his coat. Nevertheless, we had to turn the hose on him, dousing him with freezing water to rinse him down.

His aggression toward other dogs grew, worsened by the confines of the narrow, crowded docks. When he encountered another dog walking toward him, we had to take him down the walkway of a nearby slip and face away as the other dog progressed onward, holding him tightly by the leash. Yet, he seemed to know exactly when it was passing behind him and wanted to lunge, straining against his collar. All this made my heart race triple-time, but there was nothing I could do except hang on to the Flexi-lead. It was interesting to me that Gulliver was well loved on the dock despite his nasty temperament toward other canines, perhaps because he was such a sweetheart with people. He always approached with tail wagging and a Dalmatian smile for those who held their hands out. But with dogs—it was a different story entirely.

One Sunday we left the boat, navigating down the steps with our hands full of laundry, laptops, and trash. With the Flexi gripped only loosely in my fingers, I was balancing my way precariously down the narrow staircase. Two unleashed Jack

Russells suddenly bounded up our slip from a neighboring boat. (These two were affectionate, but as I often told people we met on the street who insisted on allowing their dog to approach us, "Your dog may be friendly, but mine isn't!") They came right to Gulliver where he stood on the top step, ready to greet him.

Greet them he did—by jumping off the steps and chasing after them with a loud snarl and then a stream of vicious barking. When he took off, I had the Flexi in my hand snapped down in the off position and was dragged along behind him down the steps, fighting for balance. I couldn't begin to stop his sixty-five-pound lunge.

He cut the corner of the slip and hung suspended in the air for just a second before he plunged down into the water. I called to Brad, who was busy locking the cabin's hatch, and then I tried to pull the flailing dog out of the water. The two Jack Russells had managed to make a quick exit, and dimly in the distance I could hear their owner shouting for them to come. Gulliver was wet and therefore heavy, and I was not successful in getting him up out of the water. For a moment I thought he was going to drown, as he was slipping under the neighboring boat.

Brad managed to haul him upward. Gulliver stood there shivering. Brad uncoiled the hose and began to spray him down, despite his scurried attempts to get away from the cold water. The stream of water widened as it descended over Gulliver, and Brad began to spray me. With a cry of distress, I stepped back to get away from the icy cascade and went right out into space, off the edge of the dock, just as Gulliver had done. Down I went, into the freezing 50-degree water.

Struggling, I surfaced and spat out the sea, clinging to the edge of the dock, kicking desperately. I remained hanging by my hands, the dock still high above my head, as it was low tide. I couldn't get an adequate grip. Stupidly, I kept worrying that I was going to lose my shoes if I kept kicking. And without treading water, I was going to sink.

Brad had Gulliver with one hand and me with the other, and because he was holding us both, he was unable to pull me up. Eventually I told him to put down the Flexi. Gulliver, who was whining with distress at the dock's edge, would undoubtedly go nowhere because he was worried about me. It was only then that Brad was able to hoist me up, me and all the water that had penetrated my jeans, my thick woolen turtleneck, and my heavy winter jacket. Back onto the boat I went to strip down and towel off, while Brad finished rinsing the dog. We did not speak to the owners of the Jack Russells for a very long time.

All this did nothing for the reputation of Dalmatians. Gulliver was a poster dog for all the negative ideas people already had about the breed. At the marina Christmas party that year, someone made a derogatory remark about Dalmatians and their nasty temperaments, and I started a heated argument.

I insisted that generally Dals were neither anxiety-ridden nor aggressive and walked off in a huff. When the victim of my bad temper followed me to apologize, I found myself tearfully explaining that I hadn't meant to start an argument, I just had to stick up for my dog.

• • •

At the local boating store Gulliver soon became a favorite. He accompanied us through the electronic swinging doors fearlessly, tail held high to be allowed in a place filled with two-legged beings rather than those with four, like the pet store. Patiently he waited as we walked up and down the aisles. When it was time to leave, he stood tolerantly by the register, ready for his due. And each time, the checker would pull out her bag of treats and hand the cookie to *us*, because Gulliver just couldn't resist jumping for the treat and nearly taking off your hand. No matter how hard we worked on this, he never seemed to get the hang of waiting until the cookie was in front of his nose.

And he wasn't much different with pizza crusts, or maybe that was where he got the habit. If so, our fault. As soon as he saw Brad and the big white box coming through the back door, he began to pace in circles. His nose told him what was up. And sure enough, after we demolished first one slice and then another—which we ate down only so far that a good-size piece was left—we tossed the crusts to him and he caught them with a satisfying snap, right out of the air. The click of his jaws was audible. We were nauseatingly proud of this.

Food in general brought on an extreme response, whether it was breakfast, dinner, or someone else's snack. At seven o'clock in the morning, or five o'clock in the evening, or sometimes even a little earlier, he began to pace in front of the pantry door where his kibble was kept.

"Who's *hungry?*" I would tease him. "Are you *hungry?*"

He would begin to turn in little circles, as though chasing his tail.

We were a family of three now that Gabe and Nathaniel were off to college. Maybe Gulliver took on even more importance because of the gap left in my life when mothering took up less of my time. I was reduced to reproving the kids, who rarely called home from their dormitories, and entreating them to call home. It was always up to me to initiate the phone contact, and I resented it, even though I heard other mothers complain about the same difficulties. I knew they were busy with social lives and homework, but it bothered me nevertheless. So I poured even more loving into Gulliver.

On the other hand, the kids' absence did free us up for different activities.

In addition to boating, we began to go car camping, packing in everything we thought we would need and a lot that we never did. Gulliver accompanied us as well, of course, and into the car went his supplies: dog food in a bin, his bed rolled like a sleeping bag, a thick sweater for cold nights, a chain on which to stake him out so we wouldn't have to hold him when we were assembling the tent or cooking dinner. And of course, his crate, in case he became a pest and we needed his den to calm him down and make him comfortable.

On our first foray out, to the spectacular beaches in Big Sur, we pulled in under the redwoods that would be our home for the next few days with anticipation. Even though our hands were full, the first thing we did was to install Gulliver's chain with its big spiral anchor so that he didn't need to be shut up in the car. We had a lot of work to do before dark. Nathaniel and his girlfriend had taken time out of their summer vacations and joined us but were, predictably, taking "a break" after our arduous three-hour drive.

It didn't take long before a dog passed our way along the path in front of our site. Gulliver took off and ran up against the end of his chain in seconds. Up came the anchor right out of the ground. On he went, teeth bared and growling, eyes locked onto his strolling and unaware target, in this case a small Pekinese. Fortunately, the startled and angry owner easily lifted the smaller dog in the air. Gulliver's fire quickly quenched itself when someone other than us yelled at him. He didn't look in the least bit contrite as we marched him back into camp.

He was banished to the tent and not allowed out until dinnertime.

Later, with plates sticky from steak and baked beans, he licked the paper Chinet absolutely bare, saving us a lot of scraping time as he cleaned up everything that would later have to be washed in a bucket of cold water. Apparently he thought he had been forgiven for his bad behavior—and, of course, he had.

For a few hours, Nathaniel strummed away on his guitar. It reminded me of summers at Highlawn when the head counselor would pull her instrument out of its case and get all the girls to sing, even those who were shy, and Sherlock settled in beside us to snuggle.

When we all finally went to bed, reluctant to leave the warmth of a campfire now reduced to a glowing heap of coals, Brad put Gulliver in his crate. Clad in his sweater, with a blanket draped over him, he looked snug enough. But sometime in the middle of a night, lit only by the moonshine filtering through the tent's screened window, I woke to the sensation of the nylon side vibrating against my head. Feeling my way around the tent and trying not to wake Brad, I discovered that Gulliver was shivering violently enough to shake the back wall against his crate. That was the last time we took it with us. From then on, he was wedged between Brad and me, crammed in the double sleeping bag.

• • •

When he turned six, we took him to the vet to see if there was anything we could do about his aggression toward other dogs. The days of consulting a psychic were over.

"Well, you could neuter him," she suggested.

"Would that make a difference?" I was surprised. "He's already six."

"It might help. Sometimes it does."

In desperation, we made the appointment, but I was secretly heartbroken about the idea of cutting him. He looked so natural the way he was. Probably, in reality, I just didn't want to change even one aspect about him.

"I hate the way it looks," I confided to the vet, secretly ashamed. It was obviously the practical thing to do.

She shrugged. "Well, there are Neuticles. If you want to go that far."

"What are Neuticles?"

"Fake testicles."

"You've got to be joking!" I was simultaneously horrified and curious.

"Nope. We just insert them after the real ones are removed, and they look as natural as if he had never been altered."

After a consultation with Brad, who thought I was crazy but didn't object, Gulliver received his fake set of balls. The Neuticles *looked* totally natural, as the vet had said. But they *felt* as hard as rocks. I regretted it from the moment I brought him home from the animal hospital. The entire family laughed at me. Especially Brad. And, predictably, Dawn.

It didn't help Gulliver's aggression one little bit.

• • •

Once we began to renovate the new house, I had a special bath built for him in the laundry room. It was a deep steeping tub, with a set of steps leading up to it, tiled all the way to the ceiling, and a heavy duty, restaurant-size handheld sprayer. Every visitor snickered at such extravagance, but it seemed to be the best part of the tour as we showed people around the renovation. Pat threatened to bring her troupe over weekly. Everyone had a dog who needed to be washed, and everyone wished they had a place better than the shower, with the dog at their feet, shaking his hairy coat all over their naked legs.

But Gulliver never got used to being in the water, any more than he ever got used to the pool at the other house. He stood with his face averted as the water flowed over him from the big spray nozzle and shook, vigorously, as often as possible. He always had a triumphant look when he got me as wet as he was, and I soon learned to bathe him without a shirt or bra.

When Nathaniel finished college and came home to stay with us for a while during his first job, Gulliver would bound up the steep stairs to the apartment over the garage and scarf around looking for table scraps. Table scraps were prized—more eagerly anticipated than his nightly food bowl at 5:00 PM. Nikki, Nathaniel's girlfriend, loved Gulliver and would occasionally cuddle with him on the couch as they watched DVDs after supper.

"He's the most human dog I ever met," she said. I smiled, thinking that this described Gulliver perfectly. Having both Nathaniel and Nikki around so much was another move back toward the life I had once known as a mother, a healthy upward pull. The family had increased again, and once more, a dog was at the center of it.

He continued to counter-cruise, as food was still his number one hobby, and he waited anxiously for any plates to lick after supper. He scorned nothing, not even salad, not even raw mushrooms. There wasn't a single thing he didn't like, except dry, undressed lettuce.

Once, when Brad's sister was visiting from Chicago, he raided her suitcase in search of the food he was certain was hidden in there. He discovered a treasure—a huge, oversize bar of dark chocolate. Happily, he chowed down, though Debbie caught him midway and dragged him upstairs to the kitchen.

Dark chocolate is toxic to dogs, and we quickly poured a stream of table salt down his throat to induce him to vomit. He spent the rest of the day coughing, a hoarse, sore noise that quite nearly made me regret what I had done.

After that, though, he had a persistent cough and a wheeze, especially on hot days. We associated it with the episode when he'd had the salt, but when it persisted, a visit to the vet proved us wrong.

"He's got a frozen larynx," she diagnosed, "and needs surgery to open his trachea back up so he can breathe freely again."

Then she went on to explain the side effects of the operation. "With his larynx pinned open like that, there will be nothing to keep food and water from going down into his lungs. You'll have to have him eat from an elevated bowl. And keep an eagle's eye out to make sure he doesn't aspirate anything. Especially vomit. He could get pneumonia, and that can kill—fast."

Dogs vomited all the time, I thought, especially after they ate grass, and Gulliver loved to graze.

I worried about it all, especially every time he ate or drank, but Brad said I worried about everything anyway.

The frozen larynx was the first real sign of his aging. But to my sorrow, age he did. At eleven, his muzzle began to gray. Bounding up the back hill from my office was replaced with sleeping on the couch, and he would only look up with enthusiasm when *I* came into the room, or when it was suppertime and I picked up his bowl. His haunches stiffened, and it became difficult for him to leap up onto the bed to cuddle with me at night. We settled on a new command, "Pawsers!"

for when I wanted to lift him up and get him settled on the blanket. He would rise on his rear legs and put his front feet up, and I would give him a boost. Soon he began to sit every night at the side of the bed, waiting patiently for his command and my helpful hands. I didn't have to say a word.

As he grew older, he needed to stretch out more. This made having him sleep on the bed very difficult, as there was no room for me and Brad. Gulliver settled for a new spot in the best chair in the bedroom, a thickly padded, wide bergère. There he would cuddle up, his chin on the overstuffed armrest, and watch me until his observant eyes closed. I never washed that armrest, despite the grime that accumulated over time from his chin. That reminded me of my Nana, who had had her dining room table redone but counseled the refinisher not to remove the little teeth marks along one edge, made by my father when he was an investigative toddler.

At night, before bedtime, Brad and I often sat out on the back deck, with sweaters on even in summer, as the fog that came across the mountain ridge opposite us cooled the fading day rapidly. "Nature's air conditioner," as it is known in the Bay Area, made for comfortable sleeping even when it followed a day with temperatures in the 90s.

Gulliver lay at our feet as we sat back in our wooden chairs, waiting for the sound that would call him. After a while, the coyotes began to wail back and forth to each other. He raised his head while listening to his brothers, ears pricked forward, though he did not answer them. The moon rose over the canyon. And then I thought what a perfect evening it was for us all—a dog and his family.

• • •

One late winter's afternoon, Pat called to tell me she had just been diagnosed with colon cancer. "Don't worry," she said in her typically cheerful voice, "I'm going to beat it. If you have to have cancer, this is the best one to get."

This was true, and I knew it. Caught early, colon cancer could often be curable. But my friend had waited too long, never having had the requisite colonoscopy at fifty, allowing her fear of hospitals and doctors to overwhelm her common sense. In her late sixties, she began experiencing rapidly worsening symptoms. Nevertheless, in typical fashion, she ignored them until one day she fainted with severely low blood pressure caused by internal bleeding. At last she allowed John to drive her to the hospital. But it was too late: rectal carcinoma, Stage 4.

Only a year went by, all too fast, as Dawn and I watched her slip quickly from a vibrant woman filled with laughter to a gray shadow who faded away without words. I paid frequent visits during her illness and brought the requisite casseroles and salads, but the last time I went to see her, a few days before her death, I was not able to sit and hold her hand. I was taken aback at how close death actually was. I had never had to face it head on in this way. All of my family had died quite suddenly: my mother's suicide; both my grandfathers' and my Aunt Joan's car crashes; my maternal grandmother's late diagnosis of breast cancer. And then there was my close friend Rose, who lived in New York City and succumbed to her lung cancer quickly, only a few years before Pat's passing. She had been a mother to me during the years of Nathaniel and Gabe's early childhood and, unlike other friends, did not fall out of touch when I moved to California. Her death came as a shock because she was so far away, and I did not watch the stages progress or witness her final days.

There had also been the sudden death of Diane Middlebrook, my mother's biographer, with whom I had had an intense friendship that lasted well beyond her work on the controversial book *Anne Sexton: A Biography*. There, too, I had not been able to be near her in the days preceding the end of her struggle as she lived abroad, returning to San Francisco only immediately before her death. Pat's passing was thus unique. In the space of ten years, three of my women friends had died of cancer, and then there were the other four friends who were fighting breast and pancreatic cancers as well. My father contracted prostate cancer and underwent the usual radiation therapy, which rendered him weak and angry.

It was a frightening time, yet in a different way. My own dance with death was past. I no longer had any suicidal thoughts. They had been replaced with a desire not to die from a case of cells gone awry—for the first time in many years, I just wanted to live. There was triumph in this, but loss moved through my memory, building on the sorrow that those previous deaths had brought as I mourned Pat. Once again, Gulliver fulfilled his role as therapy dog.

At her funeral, with Brad and Dawn at my side, I delivered only one of the several eulogies offered. I spoke of her generous nature and how we had become friends, so quickly. How we had shared the dogs and traveled far and wide. We had built our friendship around our animals—but then it all had moved, so quickly, so far, beyond just that. She had taught me much about persistence and humor, and that a family could be made up of friends of the same persuasion: in this case, one that was black-and-white and quite naturally bespotted.

new beginnings

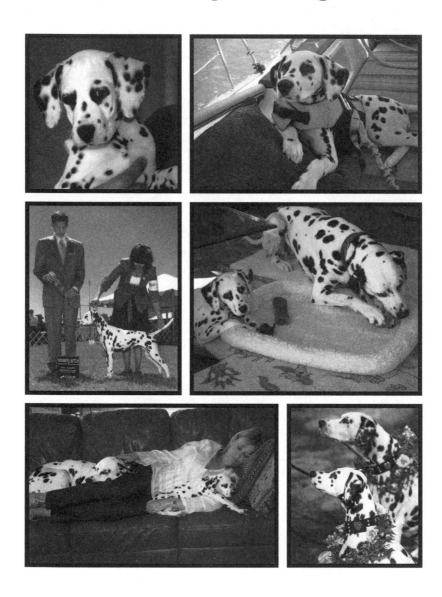

Breeze,
a.k.a. GCH SunnyOaks Saint Florian Literati's
Compass Rose

thirteen

OVER TIME, PAT'S DEATH wasn't quite so wrenching. Brad had helped. Gulliver had helped. By 2007, I was deep into work on what had turned out to be a book after all.

My days had changed radically. I was no longer living in the land of the bed or on the land of the couch—but was up on my feet again. Once again, I was back to writing about family. I began to accept that this might always be so.

I had reduced my sessions with my psychiatrist to once a week and took my medications with determined exactitude. I depended less on Gulliver for constant companionship to counter depression and more on his company just to spend my days writing, or reading a book, with him curled at my feet, rather than cuddling me on the sheets. Brad's nurturing had taken hold, and I no longer dreaded waking. Every week I improved, and even the boys were encouraged, and told me so.

Yet I worried that Gulliver had grown too isolated and wondered if that might be the reason he was so aggressive with other dogs. We couldn't exactly take him to the dog park, and even with Dawn's dogs, he looked as if he was spoiling for a fight. So we enrolled him in a class at Planet Pooch called "Grumpy Puppy," even though he was a senior citizen, and we practiced stuffing him full of cheese every time he made eye contact with another dog and didn't growl. No big surprise that he loved going to that class, but if you didn't have the cheese in your hand, he still looked as if he was going to kill the dog walking toward him.

I was also ready to have a second dog again, and Brad was quite eager for one he could call his own, just as I always called Gulliver my own, despite how much and how often we shared him. I missed the world of having a dog in the show ring, and though sailing was still a large part of our lives, I wanted more than just the wind in my hair every weekend.

We didn't know if it would be too risky to bring another dog into our home, but we thought we would at least give it a try. It would have to be a female, and a puppy, for obvious reasons. And in this way, when Gulliver was eleven, Breeze came to live with us.

It took us quite a while to find her. We had been looking for a couple of years when old friends from the show world had a new litter. Ginger and Jack were the mom and pop, Jack being Ashley's old rival and Gulliver's grandfather—in a twist typical of modern dog genetics, it was ironic that we might now take a puppy from a litter Jack had sired. He was used so frequently in breeding programs that he had become a legendary force, even though he had died several years before. Anyone who wanted to use him now had to work with frozen semen and artificial insemination. Ginger, who belonged to our old friends, Michele and Tom Wrath, had been a big winner, with many Group and Best in Specialty Show wins to her name. All in all, it was a stellar pedigree.

Dawn's house was already crowded with her three dogs, but she was ready for a new show prospect to handle. She asked me if I was interested in co-owning a girl who could live with me, while she took responsibility for the ring. I hesitated a little, wondering if I wanted to give away the right to show, but ultimately decided that with our sailing schedule, perhaps I would be more comfortable having someone else take the main chance. And it didn't hurt that she was, flat-out, a better handler than I could ever hope to be. We had renewed a friendship that had gone quiet during the years of my illness and returned to laughing once again.

Several years before, Michele and Tom had moved to the Raleigh-Durham area of North Carolina, but we hadn't lost touch, even though our contact was now mainly at the National, during Michele's trips back West for work, or at Christmastime when they came back to visit family. Dawn and I flew east to visit them and the pups. Some of my friends poked fun at me for traveling so far just to look at a puppy, but it didn't seem so far to Dawn and me. Perhaps there never is a location too far to go to for a good show prospect or a great dog. Some people even import their Dals from England, where there is a lot of interest and activity in the breed. We didn't know whether there would be a puppy we might want, but Dawn had been on Michele's list for quite a long time and thus had the first pick, after Michele chose the one she wanted to keep. North Carolina in April was beautiful. The flowering trees were just beginning to bloom pink and white, and the days were warm and sunny. We stayed for a long weekend, reveling in the weather and the new black-and-white spots.

The pups, at six weeks, were rambunctious and ready to be evaluated. We put them up on the grooming table, which made a nice, stable platform on which to stack them and set their little legs out in the square show stance. The entire litter stood up proudly and was just plain lovely. It was hard even to decide which one was first pick. We were looking for a female, with beautiful markings, a good top line—and a pretty face. I was a sucker for a pretty face.

Sometimes the head swayed me so much that I found it hard to look at other qualities, and that wasn't good. Dals are not judged for their heads, the head being only 10 points on a scale of 100, but it was always this that spoke to me—the beautifully sculpted triangular shape, the strong muzzle tipped with a moist black nose, the luminous and intelligent eyes, all of it set off by the frame of silky ears that dropped nearly to the jawline.

It was hard to judge movement at this stage, but top line, rear angulation, and shoulder layback foretold a lot about how it would develop as the months passed. As we snapped photo after photo of the puppies, talking to each other and comparing notes, we were like persnickety women sorting through sales racks in a high-end department store.

Though Dawn and I were to co-own the puppy—just as I had once done with Pat and John—Dawn let me have the final decision about which pup to choose because she would live with me. Eventually I decided on the green rickracked girl with the best markings and the prettiest head. The structure in most of the pups was so good that I was able to make my pick based mostly on cosmetics, which came as a big relief. It was like eating a whole box of chocolate truffles. I left feeling sinfully overstuffed.

She wasn't ready to go home on an airplane yet, and Dawn would be traveling nearby when she was a few weeks older, so we left her behind as we departed from North Carolina. Brad and I had begun batting names around over the phone as soon as I had settled on Green, and we decided before Dawn and I even got on the plane that she would be SunnyOaks Saint Florian Literati's Compass Rose. We had to use three kennel names because Dawn and I were co-owning, and the breeder of the litter always has his or her name come first.

Brad and I had picked the name Compass Rose because we wanted something that related to sailing, and the compass rose is a figure used on maps to display the orientation of the four cardinal directions—north, south, east, west—and the way the wind is blowing. It is usually drawn in several beautiful colors and seemed perfect for a dog we expected to be perfect. We gave her the call name Breeze, which fit with the show name so well.

Once I was back home, Brad and I felt elated as we contemplated Breeze's arrival, and yet we were also worried. Would Gulliver accept a new dog, even if that dog were a female puppy?

The three weeks passed like glue dripping from a bottle, but at last it was time for Breeze's arrival. One evening after work, we drove down to Dawn's to pick her up. Apparently she had been quiet and good in the cabin of the plane, where she was allowed to travel because she was a small dog. The flight attendants just couldn't stop cooing over her, as if she were a new baby—which she was! I marveled at the heft of her as I cuddled her in my arms, already so much heavier than only a few weeks before. New-puppy scent flooded my nose as she reached up to wash my face with her little pink tongue.

What was most striking about her at this stage was her face: her eyes had heavy mascara in a thick black rim, and the markings circling each eye flowed downward in a perfectly symmetrical triangle of pigment. There was a great deal of beauty in such harmony. With her white forehead and black ears, her face looked at bit like that of a harlequin clown. Her eyes themselves were of the darkest brown, though one of them had developed a tiny white fleck in it, which gave Dawn and me a flip of concern. A blue eye was not good, and though this wasn't blue, a fleck was a fleck, and there was nothing we could do about it except cross our fingers that the judges didn't nick us for it.

Back at our house, even though it was dark, Brad set Breeze gently down on the driveway, on leash, and waited for me to unlock the door and loose the beast. Gulliver was just plain excited to see us, the way he always was whenever we returned from being out, so even as I clipped on his lead, he was trying to scramble from his crate across the hardwood, raring to go and figure out why Brad was still outside. I held my breath, and my chest felt tight. He dragged me outside and charged across the pavement, then stopped short. After a moment, he approached, surprisingly tentatively.

He sniffed her butt.

He sniffed her nose.

He sniffed her ears.

Then he rubbed his muzzle along the length of her, as if claiming her for his very own prize. Apparently it was settled. Gulliver approved, and we could bring her inside. Breeze was officially part of the family.

We couldn't know it then, but Breeze would become like a sister to Gulliver, despite the difference in their ages. We were enlarging our family, and they were related, too, because they were cousins of a sort. But they grew closer than that, and when she came into his life, he at last learned to play. Perhaps lack of it was due to all those years of living as a single dog and not having anyone to bounce around with, but now he took to it with surprising vigor considering his eleven years.

He wasn't able to really keep up with her as she grew, but he learned a variety of clever ways that enabled them to cavort around the house together. Lying on the floor, he used the grip of his jaws and teeth to play tug, rather than the strength of his legs. Because he couldn't chase her from room to room, they developed a wacky game where she hid behind the back of the family room couch and ran back and forth, popping out from either end to surprise him where he stood with his back to the TV, swaying to the sound of her rhythm because he couldn't see her. It was a kind of stationary hide-and-seek, and both Brad and I felt absurdly pleased that he had invented it.

Gulliver didn't even get territorial about his food and ignored her when she came up to investigate his breakfast or dinner bowl, or sometimes even stepped aside to let her polish the dish after he had finished. In general, he looked very happy to have her as part of the family and spent a lot of time cuddled up with her on his bed or on the couch. It was a lesson in how even a Dal could change his spots.

Breeze was a sweet little girl who loved to snuggle with Brad as he watched television in the family room, while Gulliver went with me to the bedroom, where he reclined like a pasha among the pillows. As she grew, Brad taught her to jump up in the air for a toy—any toy—and jump she did. High. Higher. Highest. When we showed off her aerial skills, people would marvel at the heights Breeze achieved with her acrobatic body. She loved to chase a football down the steep hill to my office and grew protective of it.

Over time, we began to call Breeze "The Circle Girl" because she ran in tight little circles as she waited for her food dish, or laps around the dining room table as she trotted out to the kitchen in the morning while Gulliver was sacking me from behind, or even in the limited space of her crate when she was waiting to make a speedy exit. Each night before bed, she snuggled in her own chair, and when I came to say good night, she stood up and ground her head down in the cushion, hard, an action we began to call a "head butt." Then she would flip on her belly for a vigorous scratch, moaning all the while. Sometime after she first came to us, I described this odd behavior to another breeder, who told me that her bitch out of Jack did the same thing, and that it was a trait they had inherited from their father.

However, Breeze had one nasty habit. As she began to grow up, she decided that she hated rain, even if it was only a light patter, or even if she had on her little red raincoat with the hood. (My mother was moaning from her grave about "dog's dignity.") We didn't have to walk her because of the big back yard and so didn't realize that she thought of herself as too "delicate" to brave the elements. She hid under the eaves of the garage and came back in shaking off as if she had been in a downpour.

Once safely in the house, she would saunter about innocently, and then slide out through the dining room door, secretively and thus unnoticed, and make her deposit in the same place each time: between the back of one of the living room armchairs and the wall, on my grandmother's treasured Persian rug. Only when I smelled something suspicious while passing through the living room on the way to the kitchen or bedroom, with the scent wafting through the air as did the Stars and Stripes on the wind, did I realize she'd been at it again.

And so we developed a new nickname for her—The Sneaky Pooper. And unfortunately, we had plenty of occasions to use it. The rainy season in Northern California was long.

Per the norm in our home, the nicknames began to pile up: Miss Breeze, Breezer, Beezer, Beeze, BZ, Sweet Girl, Ms. Breezealot, Breeze Louise, Bright Eyes, and later on, Little Mama. Never Breezy, which Dawn's son had informed us meant "a loose woman." Brad developed a routine every night to entice her up onto the sofa: "Who's my good girl?" he'd croon. "Who's my pretty girl?" And he'd clap his hands together, and up she would leap to lick his ear enthusiastically, before settling in comfortably, with her head draped over his lap.

At six months, Breeze was ready to be shown, and Dawn took great pleasure in it. Finishing her championship handily, Breeze began to win as a special, and never really stopped. For a while, she and her sister, who lived in our area, dueled over Best in Breed, but eventually Breeze matured, and when she did, she often took the blue ribbon. In 2012, at the Golden Gate show where I had first sold Rhiannon's puppies via the poster on the back wall of the bench, I actually handled Breeze to a much-coveted Group placement among mostly professional handlers and some of the best dogs in other breeds in the United States, after Dawn had won Best of Breed with her and then had to leave for a wedding.

Breeze still continued to get beaten by the males because for some inexplicable reason they were often favored by the judges, and also because she had turned out to be petite. A big flashy dog had it over her many times, even though she could be more correct for type. In general, I was happy to sit on the sidelines and watch Dawn fly around the ring with our girl.

She looked like a pro, and so did Breeze. However, that excursion into the ring at Golden Gate made me realize that I did indeed miss the pulse of competition.

I thought about starting Breeze in obedience, but as she matured, she became strikingly independent, so I began to work her in Rally instead. In Rally, the handler teams up with the dog in a much less strict set of patterns than obedience, and while it could be as refined a skill, it didn't require the same exacting precision that obedience does. And part of my reluctance to tackle her CD was that I still remembered Rhiannon with such sadness, despite the many years that had gone by.

AKC had established a new title for the conformation ring, Grand Champion, and Dawn and I decided to go for it with Breeze, who was by then able to put the title CH (champion) preceding her show name. Grand Champion was harder to achieve than the previous one had been, but it didn't take Breeze long to accumulate the necessary points and majors, and soon we were using the abbreviation GCH (grand champion) for her. Just as, in another era, we would have hung our kids' new report cards on the refrigerator, after a while, another plaque hung on our dogs' accomplishment wall. And when she first came into season at nine months, Gulliver was very pleased, mounting her and humping away as if he were a young dog who had never been altered. His spirit was still intact.

• • •

When Brad and I at last decided to get married on September 19, 2009, after nine years of living together, we chose a site high in the Santa Cruz Mountains, a venue that was both beautiful and whimsical. Set on acres of naturally wild and yet groomed grounds, it had all sorts of playful touches: a miniature cottage with pint-size wooden tables and chairs made for kids and reminiscent of *Alice in Wonderland*; a small train for adults that ran from the top of the site down the steep hill to where the ceremony would be held; a renovated barn, lit golden with many candles, where dancing and cake-cutting and toasts would take place later in the evening. Dinner tables were set up beside a pond fringed with ferns and populated by mallards, and wild purple irises grew in profusion through the shallows.

Gulliver and Breeze were our ring bearers, with small velvet pillows sewn onto their collars to hold fake rings—just in case they should get away from us and take off down the steep hill where we would exchange our somewhat-eclectic vows. It wouldn't have seemed right to have a ceremony without the participation of both dogs. Encircling their necks were wreaths of coral and white lilies, in tune with the colors I had chosen for the event. Led by Nathaniel and Gabe, they went eagerly down the aisle, with Gulliver straining hard at the leash as if he couldn't wait to get to my side.

How my life had changed. With the depression banished, I was finally able to make a commitment to the man I had grown to love. Jim was married to the woman he had left me for and was at last gone from my inner emotional life, though we remained friends and saw each other occasionally with pleasure. The kids still tied us together: family died hard, and when it was he and his new wife's turn to get a dog, they turned to me to visit different golden retriever breeders with them. Once again we were the friends we'd been so many years before.

Unlike the simple ivory dress I had worn at my first wedding, this time I had picked a long white gown with a train and a full-length veil. All this was a symbol of the ways in which I was starting over again. A white dress not for the purity of my virtue, but for the pure joy of life refreshed.

Dawn and Myrna stood up for me as matron of honor and bridesmaid. At my age of fifty-four, some people might have raised their eyebrows at the elaborate event I had planned, but I didn't care. I felt certain of all these choices and took pleasure in arranging them.

We held the ceremony under a wisteria pergola that faced a small lake, where a bullfrog serenaded us as we made our vows. Over our heads a thick stand of redwood trees soared one hundred feet high, to form the sort of chapel only nature can create. We had reserved two empty chairs—one for each of our mothers—where Brad's sister laid two roses. My mother had been gone for thirty-five years, but on a day like this, I missed her. The quiet music of a harpist floated out into the still air, playing classical pieces I had chosen.

Brad and I faced each other beneath the wooden arch of wisteria decorated with coral and silver balloons, adding a lighthearted note that let our guests know that we didn't take ourselves *too* seriously. We followed a ceremony I had written from scratch, borrowing from both Christian and Jewish worlds, as well as the Native American Indian. At its center was an Old Navajo tradition I had discovered in my research for our union, which welcomed in the life-giving winds of north, south, east, and west to bless the new hearth and home being created in this quiet moment. We interwove our cupped hands one atop the other: right, left, right, left.

As each stanza ushered in a new wind, one of our children came up beside us to lay a long satin ribbon of coral or silver over our wrists. They all promised to support us, and one another, throughout the coming years, and with that, the minister tied the four ribbons into a knot around our hands. The dogs sat patiently by our sides, just the way they waited in the morning at the breakfast table or at night, hoping for table scraps.

When it came time for the kiss and the final processional, Gulliver was not able to walk up the long hill back to the reception's location, next to another pond. And so he was transported on the little train, Breeze by his side, to be taken home for his supper. He had begun to falter, just a bit. I did not want to admit that he had aged, his muzzle getting grayer, incontinence becoming more of a problem, his inability to get up on the couch or bed without serious assistance worsening. Nevertheless, he was together with us, despite these limitations. Brad continued to remind me, gently, of his age and his infirmities, pressing me to prepare for what was inevitably to come.

keeping the vigil

{IN ORDER OF APPEARANCE}

Gulliver

fourteen

AND COME IT DID, only a short eight months later, though Gulliver was a dog of gallant heart, and though he fought for every last minute of his time with us. Even as he aged, people on the street would pet him and ask how old our "puppy" was, shocked to hear that he was actually a dog well along in years. He still trotted briskly at my side, lifted his head with curiosity at every passing person, car, or dog (we had hoped age would bring toleration of other canines, but in this way, he remained as young as ever), still Lippizanered up the steep hill from my writing cottage, though perhaps more slowly than before. When we were out on the boat, even while drowsing in the sun, supremely relaxed in the way only an older dog can be, the sound of an approaching Jet Ski provoked from him the same hysterical and energetic response. In fact, Gulliver's age was truly evident to others only in the way his muzzle had started to gray, which the Dalmatian coloration hid so well—or in the slight drag of one hind foot, as he grew a bit arthritic in his left hip.

The winter after our wedding, however, just shy of his thirteenth birthday, he developed an intestinal disease called irritable bowel syndrome, not unlike that which plagues humans, which made him incontinent. Brad and I brought the entire arsenal of modern medicine to bear upon his case. I found a new veterinarian, one who specialized in internal medicine, and made an appointment. I liked Dr. Gleason when we met, liked her direct approach, and especially liked her obvious knowledge and intensive training.

When I was a child, there were no such alternatives for helping a pet live a longer life. My family outlived our dogs, mourned them, and then replaced them with others. I recalled at this time, even as I made appointments with various veterinarians to seek help with Gulliver's IBS, the way my parents had treated Daisy's leg when it twisted in the cast and crippled her for the rest of her days. There had never been any discussion about taking her back to the vet to have it reset before it was too late: dogs were dogs, and you didn't treat their maladies in an expensive, or intensive, manner. This was the way most people thought when it came to their animals.

But today's options are different, particularly when it comes to prolonging our pets' lives, contributing perhaps to a dog lover's greater and more extensive repertoire. These options, however, introduce a problem as great as the one they are meant to solve: when we can extend the life of our beloved and so push back the pain impending from loss, how do we recognize the right time to stop intervening and to let go? How do we have the courage to step up to this terrible dilemma and make certain that our choice is right and compassionate enough for the one who now depends on us so entirely?

But the time for such considerations about Gulliver had not yet arrived for Brad and me, and so, without a second thought, at Dr. Gleason's advice, we contacted a canine nutritionist from Cornell University and paid handsomely for him to prescribe a special diet for Gulliver—one with which I happily complied, baking twenty pounds of sweet potato and peeling eighty hard-boiled eggs a week. Sweet potatoes were expensive, and I drove around town looking for deals. Peeling eighty hard-boiled eggs often left me with a raw thumb that bled. I didn't care.

Gulliver was allowed to eat nothing else, not even dog biscuits, which we replaced with sweet potato chips that, not surprisingly, he loved. But the potato-and-egg diet was no panacea after several months, and the diarrhea continued as usual. Now, whenever he had an accident in the house, he looked at me with shame and humiliation in his eyes—even as I reassured him that I didn't mind cleaning it up. And this was no lie. Once he had cleaned up after me. Now it was my turn.

• • •

It was a Tuesday night, and when I had looked over to check on Gulliver in his usual place in his chair, he had thumped his tail with the energetic, whiplike action Dals use to knock over any unsecured object and perched his muzzle on the upholstered arm padded with his blanket.

But later, when I got up from watching television to let him out and give him his late-night sweet potato chip, he was nowhere to be found. I called his name over and over. Frantically running through every room, up and down stairs, I finally skidded down to find him on the outer slope of our steep backyard. His eyes glinted green in the glare of my flashlight as he looked up from eating grass. He stood amid the bed of gravel that marked the path to my writing cottage, and his attitude was one of nonchalance. I had to call him three times to persuade him to come, he who usually came bounding to the sound of my voice. How could I have fooled myself into thinking that everything was all right?

The next morning, when he went out to potty, I saw that the projectile diarrhea that had plagued him was recurring. He could not make it to the bushes at the side of the driveway, leaving across the blacktop a telltale track of bright orange poop. I sighed, frustrated. After he came in, he vomited an enormous puddle of water onto the rug, and as I sopped it up with a bunch of rags, my mind not focusing on it, my warning radar still did not sound, which was atypical of me. I had always diagnosed my sons' earaches before the pediatrician, had known when that hot spot on my skin was going to turn out to be a miserable case of poison ivy, even before it began to itch. And besides, I rationalized as I scrubbed, dogs often vomit after eating grass, which was what I had found him doing the night before. I blocked out the vet's warning about aspiration pneumonia and kept working on the rug.

Gulliver ate his bowlful of breakfast, even though he'd yakked everything up only a half hour before, something I probably shouldn't have let him do. But he was a Dalmatian, after all, so even a rocky stomach wouldn't have kept him from chowing down—and then he was ready to go out again. He might have moved slowly to the door, but it was nothing I remarked on. Only when I came back to let him in again did I realize something was terribly, suddenly, amiss. He was staggering, all four legs splayed for balance, barely able to stand.

Still in my bathrobe, I half carried him to the car, all sixty-five pounds of him, virtually stuffing him onto the floor at the foot of the seat from which he ordinarily ruled with his ears pricked as he stared out the window at the passing scenery. I drove to the vet, fast, and barely managed to get him through the door before he collapsed on the floor, lifting his head only when his name was called. The staff shook their heads. They had never seen Gulliver like this before. Neither had I.

They took him to the ICU and started an IV. Shock kept me from understanding how dire his situation was. Dr. Gleason ordered X-rays and blood panels. There were sonograms, too, but instead of being pregnant and looking eagerly for a heartbeat and all four limbs, we were searching desperately for a picture that displayed no masses, no shadows, nothing out of the ordinary. To our joy, there was nothing strange to be seen.

But our relief was short-lived, as in a matter of hours, he developed a high fever: aspiration pneumonia had joined forces with a severe gastrointestinal upset that was trashing his body with constant vomiting and continuing diarrhea. We discussed oxygen and tracheal washes and administered IVs filled with every antibiotic that money could buy. Now we would wait. They told me there was nothing further I could do, and so, still in my bathrobe, I went home, showered, and then just sat by the phone, staring into space.

Later that afternoon, when Brad and I went to the vet for a visit, Gulliver just barely managed to lift his head as we approached. He had vomited up a stone, they told me, and the night before burned across my vision like a light being turned on in darkness: his eyes reflecting green in the flashlight, where he stood on the crushed gravel path to my little cottage, as he ate grass. Had he picked up a rock by mistake? Should I have known, earlier on, that things were not right? Why couldn't I remember if he had cuddled on the bed with me that night as usual? I tortured myself with question after question and had to fight off my trembling.

I crawled into the floor-level metal cage in which he lay and put my arms around him just the way he had once curled around me where I lay on my bed of depression six years before. For three hours, Brad and I sat with him on the floor, petting his head and speaking to him in soft tones, until visiting hours ended at six.

Thursday came sunny and cool, a typical May morning. As I brushed my hair, I was certain that by the time I went to the hospital that morning, he would be better and back on the path to health. He hadn't yet had his thirteenth birthday, and Dals could live till fifteen or sixteen.

I was on my way in when the vet called me on my cell phone. I pulled over to the side of the road. She told me that his heart had stopped, and that they had managed to resuscitate him. She couldn't tell me if it would stop again. My breath came now in a ragged rhythm and the blood pounded in my head as I crashed over the rough potholed roads of the shortest route, avoiding the highway's morning rush hour, hoping for no red lights, no backed-up traffic at the stop signs. How many times had I promised him I would always be there for him at the end, my arms surrounding him?

When I arrived, the vets were all in their morning conference. In desperation, I pounded the counter until someone came out. In a minute, I was in an exam room, and he was being wheeled in on a sheet-covered gurney. He was still alive. But he didn't even need to be strapped down to make certain he didn't shift himself or fall off. He barely acknowledged me. He tried to raise his head and failed. At one time, he had licked away my tears, but my own now fell on his cheek as I bent my head to his.

I put my hand on his soft black-and-white coat. Under my hand, his breathing was labored and his eyes were at half-mast, without focus. I pressed my palm against his ribs to reassure both of us.

I called Brad.

When he came in a half hour later, Gulliver was still breathing, his eyes still half-open.

"There's a shadow over his pancreas," the vet explained to us. "We took a new X-ray this morning."

"What does that mean?" I could taste my fear.

"We don't know."

"What should we do?"

"There is the possibility of surgery," she said.

"Surgery?"

"Yes."

With that one word, she gave me hope for a miracle.

I repeated her words. "Surgery." I kept my hand on Gulliver's side, stroking the fur in the direction it ran. As always, it felt like velvet under my fingers. That had not changed.

"What kind of surgery?"

"Exploratory. It's a long shot," she said. "But I have to give you all your options."

"Why is it a long shot?" I didn't want to speak of anything negative now. We had a possibility here, and I wanted only to hear that it might work. I looked down at him.

"He could die on the table," she continued. "He could survive the surgery but die afterward. He could make it, but be in a lot of pain."

"What should we do?"

"You have to decide, soon. The surgeon needs to make up her schedule, and if she's going to put Gulliver in, she needs to know right away." She hesitated a moment and then left us, alone with the decision.

Brad and I sat back down and just looked at each other. I started to cry and couldn't stop.

"What should we do?" I asked as I blew my nose. "Should we just wait and see what happens?"

"But if he has the surgery we might know—something."

"But it might kill him."

Brad looked down at Gulliver, who lay panting now, his sides heaving with heavy effort, the IV in his arm, the tubes dangling.

"Well, he can't stay this way very long."

We sat and thought for a while. Cried harder.

"If we don't do it, you're always going to wonder," Brad said.

"He might just get well, you know. He might just heal himself."

"He might."

Silence again.

The vet put her head back in the door.

"We haven't made up our minds yet," I said. "But, if we don't do the surgery and just decide to wait, what do we do instead? Some alternative kind of treatment? Maybe with the antibiotics, all this could pass with time."

She shook her head. "I don't think that would be fair. To him." She came and sat beside me. "If you don't go with the surgery, then I think," she paused, perhaps hoping that I would come up with the word on my own. I just kept staring at her, not understanding, or perhaps not allowing myself to under-stand, what she was driving at.

"If you don't go with the surgery, then you should be talking about euthanasia."

I felt as if I had been slapped. My hands went numb, and my vision black. Her words had sucked all the regular sounds out of the room. All I could hear was silence. And then a buzz started in my ears like a hive of angry bees. Looking back, I would realize that I had been less shocked the night I was told my mother had killed herself.

How many times had I promised Gulliver that when his time came, I would not let him be in pain? How many times had I promised that I would be there to hold him in my arms and rock him out? I had never envisioned that I would be the one to initiate his slide out of this world. In my fantasy, something else was responsible. Never me.

I wasn't ready, and I never would be. I remembered my promise, but I was weak in the face of it.

"If we go for the surgery, would I be able to be in there with him?" I asked, thinking of holding him as he lay on the operating table, unconscious. I pictured how his legs would be strapped down, the tube down his throat, his tongue taped to the side. I didn't care. I just wanted to be with him.

She shook her head. "I'm sorry. No."

This meant I couldn't keep my promise if I chose surgery.

His eyes were barely open, just a tiny slit. I wasn't even sure he could see us. I called his name, but he no longer even tried to raise his head.

Brad and I sat holding hands for a long time as I continued to stroke his muzzle. It seemed there was no answer to the question of putting him to sleep. Periodically, the vet put her head in the door to see if we had come to a decision. We looked at her mutely.

I would rock him out, I had said. There will be no pain, I had said.

Left up to me, I would have sat for hours, signed a consent form for surgery, waited and waited—anything but give the signal for him to die. But he needed me to make a choice for *him*. The choice he would have made had he possessed a real voice, and spoken a language we could understand. This was the very first time I was unable to hear the voice I had created for him guiding me, and so it was up to me to make the decision now. I owed him this, not only because I had promised, but also because this was part of the covenant between him as my dog and me as his keeper. I would do for him what he could not do for himself. This time it was my turn to bear the pain in order to alleviate it.

"We'll never know if we don't do the surgery," Brad said.

"Will it matter? Will anything matter once he's gone?"

Brad didn't answer.

We just sat. An hour passed. Two hours. I kept talking to my love, but he did nothing except breathe in a shallow fashion, with great effort.

"We have to let him go," I said at last. "I think he's in pain." He reminded me of my own children, young and sick with the flu, only Gulliver couldn't tell me where it hurt.

Brad dropped his head.

I went to the door of the room and called out. After a minute, the vet put her head in the door.

"We've decided to let him go." I could barely speak.

"I'll be right back," she said.

I don't know how much time passed then. I just sat there, calling to him, trying to make him see me, but he I wasn't sure he could.

She returned with two syringes in hand.

Quickly, sensing how hard this was for us, she sat down on the bench beside me. Brad stood on the other side of the stretcher.

"I have one shot for tranquilizing him, which will make it easier on him, but it may make him feel strange, so he might stir, try to move," she explained. "And then I'll inject the other, which will stop his heart."

I wanted to cry out, "Wait!" But I just wrapped my arms around him, as I had promised. I began to rock him, just a little, the way a mother would her child.

The vet picked up the first needle and injected it into the IV line. Sure enough, Gulliver stirred and tried to rise. "It feels strange, doesn't it, old boy?" she comforted him. "Relax."

I pulled my arms tighter around his neck.

"Easy, easy," I crooned. He pulled himself up onto his elbows and looked around. I hoped he could see that I was there. I hoped he recognized me. And then he sank back down, into my arms once again, and his eyes closed.

She injected the second syringe. I continued to hold him, my arms a cradle around his head. And after a few seconds his breathing stopped and he went totally still. Suddenly, he felt soft, and he relaxed in my arms. I looked into his eyes then and saw that he was gone.

"So fast!" Brad cried. "It's over so fast?"

I nodded. I was sobbing now. I couldn't speak at all.

"I should have warned you how quick it could go," said the vet.

I kept sobbing. I didn't let go of him.

"Could I clean him up?" I asked, after a while. "I'd like to clean him up before you take him away."

She nodded, as if this weren't an unusual request. "I'll get some solution and some cloths."

She returned quickly and then left us with our sorrow.

The cries came out of me on their own accord. I did something I had never done before, not even at my mother's funeral:

I keened. It was a deeper sort of hurt, unexpected in a way hers hadn't been because she had danced with death so often. Gulliver had been valiant, had tried so hard, despite the discomfort, despite the humiliations of his body, to lead a good and vibrant life. And then, too, he had taken care of me, whereas I had taken care of my mother, and that made all the difference now.

After a while, I picked up the spray bottle and began to wash him down, where the IV had been, where the Betadine had stained his skin, where the urine was left from his final accidents. There were no words. There were only my hands on his still, warm body. Only the tears streaming down my face, stinging my eyes. After a while, I pulled his sheepskin blanket up around his shoulders. I kissed him and pulled him into my arms once again.

Brad was still sitting in stunned silence. I knew the people in the waiting room could hear my noisy sobs, but I didn't care.

We sat with him for another half hour, I think. I didn't look at my watch. I kept stroking him. I didn't know how to stop.

But at last it seemed that it was time to leave. I didn't want to see him stiffen and the life that was still there, such as it was, go out of him with finality.

I went to the door again and called for the vet. "You won't just put him in a heap somewhere?" I asked. "You'll keep him covered with his blanket?"

"He has to go into the freezer," she answered, apologetically. "Just until they come to get him. I'm sorry. They should be here by this afternoon. But I'll make sure his blanket stays with him." She reached down and unbuckled his collar and handed it to me. I gripped the leather in my hand: his life, his death.

afterward

{IN ORDER OF APPEARANCE}

Breeze

Mikey

fifteen

I WAITED, WITH SORROW and anxiety, and finally in a few weeks, the animal hospital called to say his ashes were ready to come home.

The day was sunny, just like the day he died. I was teary before I even got through the door. The receptionist bent to a cabinet beneath the desk and pulled out a little pine box with a brass plaque that had his name stamped on it. I cradled it against my chest, and we drove home again. As simple as that.

Breeze greeted us at the door and examined us both, hard, with her nose, undoubtedly smelling the vet's office on us again, and suspicious as to why we still didn't have Gulliver with us. She had continued to look for him, day after day, wondering why she was suddenly eating out of his food bowl at the raised stand I couldn't bear to see empty. Why he wasn't there to play hide-and-seek around the couch. Why he wasn't there to curl up with, sated, after dinner. Or to romp up and down the hill with first thing in the morning after breakfast. She was depressed, too, picked at her food, and just lay on the rug, facing the back door, as if she expected him to come in at any moment.

The days went on.

I didn't know what to do with the box of ashes; I couldn't figure out where to put it: the mantel just didn't feel right, but eventually I put it up on a bookshelf in the family room because that was where he had spent most of his time in the later years, sleeping on the sofa. Not the right location, but the only one I could think of.

When I was very young, my family used to drive past cemeteries on the way to other spots. My sister and I always held our breath as we passed, squealing about "catching cooties" from the dead. Pet cemeteries were the worst, with their monuments and markers, and we always made fun of them. I had allowed Gulliver's body to be cremated because I didn't know what else to do, and I didn't want to bury him on our property because if we moved, he would have to be left behind. There wasn't a pet cemetery near us, and he would have felt too far away even if there had been.

Increasingly, I wasn't happy with his location. I wanted a place that was less prosaic than a bookshelf. More special. Something that appropriately represented my feelings for him. A friend suggested creating a garden for him, and this seemed a brilliant idea, to create a place that would be the home for his urn and that would flower with blooms during the spring and summer.

I knew just the spot. Behind the house there was a little space that got a bit of sun during the day. It had a chaise longue for sitting in and daydreaming, right under three enormous Monterey pines. On windy days, the branches soughed in a comforting manner, and the needles that dropped during the autumn months left a soft bed underfoot. In spring, the dust of the pollen fell like yellow rain, and I would sneeze when

I visited. The tiny pond I had built there made a patter as water spilled from the mouth of a small bronze frog. I bought several large terra-cotta pots and planted them carefully, and then piled round gray landscape stones to create a little platform for him.

But then I realized I couldn't put a wooden box outdoors, susceptible to our rainy winters. And so I found myself on the Internet, doing something I would never have anticipated back in those days when my sister and I held our noses while passing cemeteries: I searched for animal cremation urns. Not surprisingly, I found quite a lot of them, and I spent a long time deciding which would be the best. At last I settled on one that was a deep green marble, with a classic design, and of a size big enough to hold a dog of sixty-five pounds. That was how they were sold: by the weight of the body. I thought about his body again, how still and soft he suddenly became when the last breath stopped midway in his throat. I ordered the urn and had Gulliver's name engraved on it. It took only a week for it to be delivered.

One day in late June, while Brad was at work, I opened Gulliver's small pine box. Somehow I felt the act of transferring his ashes was private—just between him and me. Inside there was only a clear plastic bag of gray dust. I picked it up and held it in my palm. It was cool to the touch and squished in my fingers.

My hands shook as I placed the bag that now held my dearest friend into his final resting spot. Carefully, I pushed it down into the mouth of the urn and settled him in. Then, along the edge, I squirted out a thick line of the marine adhesive Brad always used on the sailboat, sealing the urn shut and protecting Gully from the rains that would come in October.

I set it down on the platform I had built in the garden, situating it carefully so that the inscription was immediately visible as you came into the space, his name and his dates engraved in a subtle gold—all that I had wanted. I didn't want "beloved," or "in our hearts," or anything that might seem maudlin. I hadn't even put down his show name when I ordered it because, in the end, he was just "Gulliver."

I rummaged around in the garage until I found the dog angels that Dawn had given me when I had to put Rhiannon and Tia to sleep. Flat and cut from wrought iron, they were attractive, generic-looking dogs, in profile, with small wings coming off their backs. I had never used them, perhaps because my guilt over Rhiannon and Tia's death had been so keen for so long. They were rusty now, but that didn't matter. I only wished I had one for Gulliver. Their stakes sunk deeply down into the soil, and soon they were flying next to his urn, keeping him company.

I would never again pass a pet cemetery and hold my breath.

• • •

I visited him every day and told him everything we would have discussed if he had still been here: what was going on in the house, what was happening between Brad and me, how Breeze was doing without her big brother, how my work was progressing. Everything. I touched the cool marble the way I had once stroked his warmth and told him how much I loved him.

A month passed. The impatiens I had planted there bloomed pink and ivory; the lobelia and alyssum hung over the edges of the pots in a froth of blue and white. I came in the mornings after breakfast, and in the evenings before supper. I hung his collar on the handle of my purse and felt that he went everywhere with me. He was as full in my mind as he had been in my life. With time, I grew afraid that the collar might drop off, and so I reluctantly removed it and hung it on the photo of him I kept beside my bed—the photo to which I said good night every time I turned out the light, stroking his soft face, now behind glass.

And I began to wait for the pain to subside.

sixteen

I FORCED MYSELF TO work. But grief still reigned. Being unable to work on anything new that was creative and connected to the actual process of writing scared me, reminded me of the time when Gulliver was all that stood between me and death.

I wasn't able to go down to my office. It was too filled with the memories of him curled up in the blue armchair. If I'd had a nine-to-five job, I would have left home and gone somewhere that wasn't filled with memories. Worse still, writing required you to open yourself up. Without that surrender to the unconscious, imagination refused me. And so instead I just sat at the little desk in the kitchen where I ordinarily paid the bills.

Yet, to be without memories didn't feel right either, and so I began to hang up photos of Gulliver, taping his many faces onto the cherry cabinets that held my cookbooks over the desk. There he was in profile. Or lying snugged up on the boat with his head on his paws in his life jacket. Looking up at me, adorned with the flower wreath he wore as a ring bearer for our wedding. Cuddling at Christmas with Brad and me, on the green sofa. At a show, with Butler and Ashley, after one of her big wins in Brood Bitch. In bed, his head on my chest, my hand draped around his sturdy neck.

Every week, I added a new photo.

He looked down over me, still keeping watch. Someday, I would take down the photos, and this period of mourning would be at an end. Someday he would live on only in my heart.

We weren't really able to hold a service for Gully until a few months after he had passed. And then we took the sailboat out to "Gulliver's Beach" at Paradise Cove, both places that now seemed so right. And right there that day, opposite his beach at Paradise, we dropped the hook. The hours passed until we waited for precisely the right time. At sunset, we went up onto the deck to say our true good bye. It was a calm evening and the boat barely rocked, just the current passing, giving us a stable footing at the bow.

I had brought along a carefully selected bunch of flowers, and as the sun set, casting an orange light over the small waves, I began to drop them alongside the boat, into the water.

"This is lavender," I told him, throwing a handful of the fragrant stems over the side. "Lavender because you loved to romp through the plants in my garden and come in smelling of the musky scent.

"And this is a rose, from the bush Dawn gave us right after you died.

"This is a yellow daisy because it was my Mom's favorite flower, and I know she would have loved you as much as I do—and because I am sure she is here with us right now.

"This is alyssum, white, for the purity of your heart.

"And bleeding heart—purple for your courage, and red for your love.

"This is a pink rose from the arbor that arched over the back door to the house, your favorite way to come in to get your supper at night."

I dropped the last bloom, and Brad and I just stood there with hands linked and tears falling, as the flowers lay on top of the waves without sinking.

They passed the stern, carried away from us on the current until they became mere specks in the distance—floating straight toward the beach that we had named as his.

seventeen

IN NOVEMBER, THE RAINS began and the flowers in the garden died. Gully's urn looked forlorn. I couldn't bear the idea that he was cold and lonely out there now that I couldn't sit in the lounge chair and visit, and so I brought him inside, setting the urn on my desk next to my computer. Only Myrna and Brad understood my reaction, and I didn't admit it to Dawn, who was so practical and pragmatic and might have seen it as silly. I didn't want to hear any jokes about what I had done.

A few more months passed. The loss did not ease but kept changing shape. I remembered him with joy and sorrow, but no longer with the shocked pain his death had originally brought, no longer with the deep and dark emotion I had felt in those days after I took him from our lives with my decision. No longer with the anger I had originally felt toward God or life or fate or whatever was responsible for his untimely death. Even the uncertainty about the decision to put him to sleep began to pass. It was taking time to go through the many stages of grief, as much time as I had imagined it would when I had worried about losing Gulliver in years past. The days moved by slowly.

And then that winter, just as the publication date for my next book arrived, loss descended once again. This time it was Myrna. Myrna, who had stood up as my bridesmaid just one year before. Now, terrible night sweats plagued her, though at sixty-three, she was past menopause. At last, she consulted with her doctor. After an MRI determined that there was some kind of a tumor in her abdomen, the subsequent PET scan "lit up," an indication that the growth was indeed malignant. We all sat back in shock.

The diagnosis: metastatic melanoma. The tumor was the result of a small, malignant lesion on her ankle ten years back, one which the doctors had promised her was entirely eradicated. She hadn't had to have chemo then; clean margins had been obtained, and the lymph nodes were clear. No one mentioned that small determined cancer cells might slip past the nodes and reseed themselves elsewhere.

After a biopsy, her condition was categorized as Stage 3B. Melanoma, her oncologist explained, was a sneaky kind of cancer. Not something easy to cure, as was that of the colon. Pat had died because she had waited too long to respond to her symptoms.

But Myrna hadn't avoided doctors and had had her regular mammograms, her regular checkup with the dermatologist to make sure that the original site on her ankle was inactive. Under the pall of her diagnosis, my winter grew even bleaker, filled by gray skies and rain. I didn't allow myself to think of the worst: what would I do if the friend who understood me so well died?

May rolled around, and with it, the first anniversary of Gulliver's death. I spent a lot of time sitting outside with his urn, back in the garden now. I mooned around, sadness revving up in me, tears returning, inundated with flashbacks from the day he died, the terrible act of putting him down. And here was Myrna, too. For a while, it all seemed too much to bear. At night, I couldn't succumb to the undertow of sleep.

However, Dawn temporarily shook me out of my worry by suggesting that we breed Breeze when she came into season again: perhaps by the time the puppies were born in the summer, nearly a year and a half after Gulliver's death, I would be ready for a new dog, and this time maybe I would decide to show it; perhaps it would cheer me up as I sat there afraid for my dear friend. But part of me worried that a new puppy would just make me miss Gulliver more. It would be part of letting go, part of putting him to rest at last.

And so, I wasn't sure I would be ready.

Nevertheless, I was willing to try, just as I was trying to be cheerful whenever Myrna and I went out to lunch. Now it was my turn to keep her company through a crisis, as she began her rounds of chemo and blood transfusions. Sometimes we sat together in the hospital and I read to her as she lay with tubes running into her, carrying the precious fluids that might save her. We didn't talk about what would happen if none of it worked. Sometimes, in the late afternoon, if we were feeling sleepy, we both closed our eyes and took a nap.

The chemo was grueling, and most of the time, she was exhausted. I couldn't visit her as often as I wanted, and so we often spent an hour or so on the phone during the evenings. In some odd way, it helped her if she could recite her symptoms to me, over and over again, like a mantra, as she tried desperately to exert control over all that was happening to her. Slowly, her strength drained from her—but never her spirit. Generous and empathetic to a fault, she always insisted, no matter how poorly she felt, on knowing what was happening to me—with Brad, with work, with the kids, with the dog. And with the possibility, which now presented itself, of having another litter. And in this way, the subject of puppies came up, despite Myrna's bleak outlook. I retreated into the idea of new life as a way of avoiding what was truly threatening me.

. . .

This time around, however, it would be a bit more complicated than it had been with Rhiannon and Ashley. For one thing, I no longer had the equipment required for having puppies. And if I were lucky enough to have a show candidate, I had discarded all the paraphernalia from my show career. All my suits and treat pouches. All my show leashes and collars. All my obedience equipment, given to me by my father over the years as Christmas gifts, which reminded me, silently, of Rhiannon: out had gone the expensive broad and high jumps in their nifty canvas bag; into the Dumpster went the custom-made wooden dumbbells and also the metal articles, never touched because we never got to the level of Utility Dog. I had given away my whelping box and weaning pen and all my breeding and whelping books. It was a stupid thing to have done, but I never anticipated that I'd be back in the ring again, much less having another litter of puppies.

But there was another problem: Breeze hadn't been in season for over eighteen months, in contrast to a female dog's normal cycle of six. Dawn and I took her over to Dr. Janice Cain—who had followed Ashley throughout her artificial insemination and her pregnancy—to see whether Breeze had an issue. The report came back clean: nothing to worry about. Dawn and I shook our heads and used the extra time to figure out a suitable sire. Without realizing it, I was choosing to bring a waft of life back into my own, which had grown so dark since Gulliver's death. I had been lucky enough to have a book published during that time, but it had paled next to the loss of Gulliver and the onset of Myrna's illness.

We had slowed down on entering Breeze in a lot of shows, as we were anxious for her first litter. She was nearly three, but we decided that since she wasn't in season anyway, we might as well take her to the National. I wasn't able to attend that year due to publicity for my latest book, but Dawn would go, show Breeze, and look for a suitable "husband."

In May, on the day before the she was due to fly out, I found a brown smear on the sheet we used to cover the blanket on the bed. With impeccable timing, Breeze had finally decided to give in to nature. Once there—with Breeze wearing her seasonal panties—Dawn observed the dogs quietly from the sidelines and came up with her choice: GRCH Cranbrooke's Back to the Future, "Mikey," a dog who lived in Canada.

I had my reservations about him, despite his great win record and offspring who had also done very well. One of my main concerns was that he was too colorful, but Dawn was more focused on top line and croup. Though Breeze's were good, they could be improved on. So I relented, and Mikey was the lucky boy.

On the eighth day of her estrus cycle, which happily fell on the last day of the classes, we dispatched Breeze with Mikey—in his very own motor home—up to Ontario, to the home of Doug and Linda Taylor. Dawn waved good-bye to Breeze as they all drove away in the RV, while I, back at home due to my book's publication events, had my own misgivings. It was not easy to send my baby girl off with people I had never met, all in the name of a litter of puppies.

The Taylors treated Breeze as if she were a patient in the fat cats' wing of the hospital. She was ensconced in her very own private room, on her very own overstuffed armchair, looking out her very own window at the comings and going of the other dogs. The Taylors had a three-acre lot, but she couldn't run free because of her "condition." She was walked hourly—better than she got at home—and was, in general, treated like a queen.

On the first day that they attempted a breeding, Breeze had no interest and took off, anything to get away from Mikey— even though he thought she smelled pretty good. But on the second day, she stood up proud and ready and flagged her tail to the side, indicating that she would stand and make it easier for him. The tie lasted half an hour, and when she got tired, she tried to lie down, but Doug caught her and sat her across his lap, where she promptly fell asleep. So much for my concern that, as a "maiden bitch," she would be resistant.

On the third day (two days apart is generally considered the appropriate timing for an optimal breeding), Breeze was more than ready, and they were joined rump to rump in a matter of minutes.

A week after she left on the Taylors' RV, she arrived at the San Francisco airport. Dawn and I went down to pick her up at United Airlines cargo; after a five-hour flight, she was waiting there in her kennel, scratching hard at the door to be let out.

Brad and I watched her daily, wondering whether we were imagining the symptoms, whether we could trust Mother Nature, *or* a dog.

"Are there puppies inside? Is anything growing in there at all?" we asked each other.

Gestation is sixty-three days long in a dog, and we couldn't get an ultrasound to see whether or not any embryos had settled inside the horns of the uterus until the twenty-fifth day or so. We were nervous and eager. Breeze played hide-and-seek in a dark closet, experimenting with nesting perhaps, or else just teasing us. We began to hope.

In the excessive fashion so typical of me, I quickly ordered four books on canine pregnancy and on how to whelp a litter. Brad said it was probably like riding a bike, but I ignored him, and, reading avidly, I did learn things I'd never heard before or had indeed forgotten: the books said that wet and sloppy kisses spelled pregnancy, especially from a girl who had held herself just a little bit aloof from me. So, too, the way her nipples were rapidly becoming more swollen and prominent. And then there was something that looked to be morning sickness, as she rejected all food.

However, each of these signs was so subtle and subjective—and I also knew there was the very real possibility that she was having a "false" pregnancy (not uncommon in dogs), and that all these symptoms might be signs of nothing. Daisy had once swelled up as if she were full of pups and then endured a labor that lasted for hours and produced nothing. My father had taken her to the vet, where a standard X-ray revealed no puppies.

The day for the ultrasound arrived along with a lot of anxiety on my part. Dawn and I took Breeze to Dr. Cain, even though it was a fairly long drive across the bay to San Ramon. It seemed a wise idea to have the best doctor available when determining whether or not there were puppies by sonogram: an expert at reading the grainy gray screen could actually give you a puppy head count. So here I was again, my heart loud in my chest—but this time not for my own pregnancy.

The room was dark, and Breeze lay in a padded cradle on her back, gel on her pink belly, me restraining her head. The screen lit up with strange black, white, and gray shadows that I couldn't interpret. And then Dr. Cain said, "Here are two her body has resorbed. The sacks are empty."

My palms started to sweat.

And then she moved on. "But here are two more, these have heartbeats."

I kissed Breeze's nose from where I stood, holding her head, grinning down at her. And then there were two more heartbeats and then another and then another: six viable fetuses. Even Dawn had a smile on her face. Dr. Cain made a quick calculation with her calendar: Breeze was due on July the fourth. We were going to have a litter of fireworks puppies!

PART VIII

we wait

{IN ORDER OF APPEARANCE}

Breeze . . .

and six pups

eighteen

BRAD AND I BEGAN to watch Breeze in earnest, and I reported each development to Dawn, to Michele, and to Myrna as well. Just like any pregnant woman, Breeze threw up her breakfast. When she stopped doing that, she began to act as if we hadn't fed her in a month. She mooned around the countertops and dinner table, looking for freebees. I didn't want her to get fat, so I resisted her increasingly affectionate ways. If she'd been cute before, now she was even cuter.

About every fifth day, Brad and I positioned her with her silhouette outlined against the pale blue wall in the dining room. We were as obsessed as the parents-to-be who keep taking pictures of the wife's increasingly distended stomach. We put the photos up on the computer and ran them like a slide show, and soon the distinction between before and after was unmistakable. She didn't have a belly button to measure by, but one of the spots on her lower left flank stretched bigger and bigger and bigger. Her teats were getting ready for milk and hung down pendulously. She began to look like a small cow—big body, small head.

Even before Breeze began to nest in earnest, I did. I ordered the biggest-size whelping box, complete with a large weaning pen, and when Breeze tried it on for size after it had arrived, she looked like a peanut against the side where she had curled. Brad looked at me dubiously. It was obviously made for a larger-size breed—like a Newfoundland—and Breeze could hardly get over the side to jump in. I made Brad saw the opening down so that she wouldn't scrape her belly.

I unearthed an antique and unreliable scale (soon to be replaced by the kitchen digital) and found an old plastic pencil case full of hemostat clamps, leftover rickrack, old K-Y jelly, and surgical gloves. I threw most of the old out and bought new. Not because I needed to, but because it seemed right that Breeze should have the best.

From the backyard storage shed, I pulled out a big cardboard box marked "Puppy Supplies." As I unpacked it, I realized that the handwriting on the side was Pat's, running slightly downhill, but bold and unmistakable in any case. I stopped and stood in silence for a moment, remembering the litter we had raised together and all the good times we had. I thought of her often but perhaps missed her even more at a time like this. She would have been so excited about Breeze's pregnancy. We would have been shopping for all this together.

And of course, thinking of Pat brought me back full circle to thinking of Myrna, and I felt my fear and worry return once again. Myrna and I were talking on the phone every night, and despite her "chin up" attitude, it was clear to me how quickly her symptoms were worsening. She listed them over and over: the fevers and the chills, the weakness, the pain in her side—as if talking about all this in detail would give her control over the cancer. In turn, I pushed away my own fear for her and regaled her with tales of my crazy shopping list for Breeze, hoping to distract her. She did laugh and counseled prudence—advice I ignored.

I wasn't leaving anything to chance, any more than a newly pregnant couple would have waited to buy their crib or changing table until the week before the scheduled arrival of their darling. And so, at Costco, I selected a huge pack of white towels that I then bleached two times, rinsed three, and folded and stacked in a wicker basket. A set of sheepskin rugs and special puppy pee pads arrived from Canada, along with a newfangled ceramic warming lamp to replace the old red heat lamp, a kind that had fallen into disfavor since Ashley's litter due to its flammable qualities. I bought clean brown paper at U-Haul to go under Breeze as she delivered, so that I could pull the sheets off as they got messy, like tablecloths in a restaurant.

We needed a warming box to hold the puppies and to keep their temperature stable while Breeze was occupied with de- livering another pup, or if we had to make an emergency jump to the vet midway through her labor. Target had it—a shallow plastic storage box—along with the soft hand towels I would use to line it. I used a photo in my enormous emergency book on whelping premature puppies as a guide to the optimal size. I drew the line, however, at an oxygen tank for premies, when I learned it would cost over $400.

Little by little, I was remembering what to assemble, what I would need, all the while reading the whelping books that helped me see what I would have to do once again. More stuff: forceps to crush the umbilical cords, which seemed a better al- ternative to dental floss. Surgical scissors to cut them. A heating pad for the warming box, and a hot-water bottle, too, because I wasn't sure which would work better. A bulb syringe to suction the babies' noses and mouths from the liquid and mucus that could fill their lungs as they came down the birth canal. Big black trash bags. Paper, pen, clipboard, and charts designed by Brad, to record the time and order of whelping, the weights of the babies, and any other notes we wanted to make.

At the pharmacy, I filled my shopping basket with Betadine, rubbing alcohol, hand sanitizer, and a rectal thermometer. At the sewing supply store, I chose rickrack in six bright colors to adorn their necks so that we could tell who was who. A feeding tube, just in case Breeze's milk was insufficient, and a can of special goat's milk formula that I drove to four stores to find. On and on it went, the costs mounting. I was preparing as if I were the one going to have the babies. And this was my layette: the crib, the swaddling clothes, the receiving blankets, and the onesies.

· · ·

A month before Breeze was due to deliver, I hired a doggie "midwife" service. WhelpWise would be there to guide me through the delivery—after all, it had been ten years since my last litter, and twenty-eight years since my last baby. As I spoke to the owner, Karen, over the phone, she went through the process with me in detail. She wanted me to understand, precisely, the way her midwives worked to help their clients deliver healthy litters. Her expertise was apparent. She had been an obstetrical nurse in the operating rooms of several large hospitals—the human sort—before beginning her own practice with canines. All the staff at WhelpWise were professionals skilled at helping dogs to whelp successfully not only through normal deliveries, but particularly through those that ranged from difficult to emergency situations. After spending two hours on the phone with Karen, I knew I would be in good hands, and Dr. Cain had personally recommended her the day of our ultrasound.

All these preparations were new ways, to me, to ensure a smooth delivery that came with healthy, kicky pups. I was certain that WhelpWise would prove invaluable, especially if Breeze's labor slowed or stopped and we had to have an emergency C-section.

Three weeks from the due date Karen and I had calculated, I phoned to let her know that Breeze and I were getting close to being ready to start practicing with necessary equipment. Through the postal service, she sent a giant cardboard box filled with an assortment of confusing machines and pieces and electric cords: a round flat sensor that attached to a small recorder that attached to a base unit the size of the old hard drive that my computer used back in the eighties. All of it to measure her uterine contractions. The sensor plugged into a gadget that interpreted the data and sent it via a modem line to their base station so that it could all be interpreted. The equipment would tell us if Breeze's contractions were growing weaker during labor, a sign she was tiring, or approaching uterine inertia.

A Cesarean section, if done in time, might rectify any of these problems—hopefully, before either a puppy or Breeze died. I didn't want to think about death any more than I already was with Myrna, and so I blocked such possibilities from my mind and just focused on how all this equipment and advice would provide invaluable assistance. I was feeling a little nervous about this whelping—as the years had passed, it seemed as if I had become even more of an inveterate worrier. This time the way I handled that was to begin practicing, which, as it developed, was not at all easy.

I sat down and went through all the directions impatiently, and then had to start over, more carefully. There was a fetal monitor, a Doppler that would amplify the pups' heartbeats and let us know if one in particular needed immediate help because its heartbeat was either slowing or hastening beyond the normal limits. However, it was the unexplained, mysterious sheaf of papers that had black-and-white diagrams of a dog's belly with numbers written on them that stumped me. It reminded me of the connect-the-dots game I had done as a child, only it turned out to be a lot more complicated.

Dr. Cain's office was too far away and open only nine to six, if there were any kind of emergency during delivery. So Dawn and I escorted Breeze to our local neighborhood vet together. We felt he was quite competent, and the office was staffed twenty-four hours a day. An emergency Cesarean section in the middle of the night was something they ought to be able to handle, or so we hoped. At this appointment, it was time to do an X-ray that would give us a final headcount, because by now, the bones of the babies should be visible, from skull to tail. In the case of uterine inertia, when the puppies stop descending from the uterus, knowing the numbers would help us decide whether she needed a C-section.

I was as filled with anticipation as I had been at the ultrasound. Dr. Dickley, the vet, looked pleased with Breeze's development and asked me for dates: when had she been bred the first, second, and third times? Ever the efficient mom, I had brought my calendar with me so that there would be no question.

I put Breeze up on the table, turned her on her side, and left the room as they shot the X-ray, but when they put the films up on the light board, nothing showed. At all. No spines, no legs, no toes. I looked on in disbelief.

"Maybe she resorbed them," observed Dr. Dickley calmly.

I wasn't calm at all. Dawn, too, looked dismayed.

"We had heartbeats just a month ago," I said with despair.

"Maybe your dates are off?" he suggested. "Come on, let's do an ultrasound."

Back up on the table, this time in a cradle, Breeze on her back this time. And then suddenly, there they were again, spinning head over foot, side to side, paws and arms and legs and spines and heads all visible. It had just been too early, I realized with relief. As usual, I had rushed things as a way of dealing with my worry.

"Come back for the X-ray in four days," Dr. Dickley pronounced. "The ones we are seeing are certainly viable. Good strong heartbeats. You need to count your dates again."

I went home and worked with the calendar, this time counting from the second time she had been bred rather than the first. I also factored in the new information Dr. Dickley had given us that embryos could sometimes float around, fertilized, for as much as seven days before settling down to embed in the uterus. There was actually far more variability than I had realized when I had counted the days till delivery. I called Karen at WhelpWise, and we recalculated Breeze's dates with the new information. She reassured me with the news that she had been through all this before and had yet to deliver a litter of puppies who came without bones.

With both Rhiannon and Ashley, we had done none of these tests. We had just waited for nature to take its course. And it had all worked out fine. But this time around, it seemed risky to me. I was more anxious, an older mother. There was better medical information and assistance available to us, and it seemed smart to use whatever we could to ensure both Breeze's health and the puppies' as well. I just hadn't planned on it to backfire.

Now time seemed to move excruciatingly slowly. Brad and Myrna were especially supportive, but I just couldn't relax. Dawn was dealing with the uncertainty a different way: she blocked it out and didn't want to hear anything negative. Michele was quiet, but reassuring.

The fourth day arrived, but there were only a few faint visible spines and maybe a single skull. Once again, we did a sonogram, and there they all were, cartwheeling around, moving in an array of life. "It must still be too early," Dr. Dickley advised.

This time, I made the appointment for five days later. This time, bones would show or they wouldn't. I kept having nightmares of delivering jelly babies. Karen and I recalculated again.

Despite the anxiety, I told myself to be sensible and get everything ready. Breeze's time was only a couple of weeks away, and I needed something to do while I waited. So I demolished the guest room. Packed away were the new comforter and pillow shams I had just bought for the bed. Up to the attic went the good lamp, and out came a worn old thing with a peeling shade that gave brighter light.

And underneath it all was the wish, made of magic, that she was carrying a show boy for me, a boy to whom I could give all the love I had once given to Gulliver. Not a replacement for him, but a way of going back to loving once again.

• • •

Before the next X-ray, I began to practice with both the uterine monitor and the Doppler, as WhelpWise had suggested, even though it was a bit early to be monitoring. Over time, as I grew proficient with the equipment, I found the hour-long sessions calmed me. If I could hear heartbeats, then surely those babies were alive and kicking. Surely they must have the beginnings of bones. Surely the upcoming test in a few days would show us what I wanted so badly to see.

But the first time Breeze and I tried the monitor, it was a disaster. Just getting the tethering straps untangled was a nightmare, and, to my chagrin, I had to enlist Brad's help. Eventually, we finally got it all arranged correctly. But then Breeze refused to hold still and kept rolling around onto her back, throwing her huge belly up into the air. At last I convinced her that lying on her side wasn't so bad when you got your head stroked endlessly, but just when we'd gotten about twenty good minutes of timing under the belt, Brad came through the door and she scrambled up, having had enough of it all, and went to get her ball.

So, I gave up and the next night went back to try to record and listen. Using the monitor went more smoothly, and so I dared to try the Doppler. Itchy to hear those heartbeats, I needed to learn how to time them with my watch to obtain baseline figures for each one. Those figures would later tell us if a puppy had gone into distress.

This night, Breeze lay on her side quietly and snoozed while I stroked the sides of her abdomen with the square head of the Doppler, looking for some sign of life. Nothing. My hands grew sweaty, and it became harder to push the Doppler around. After a while, my fingers began to ache as I kept pushing the head into her side, down below her ribs, up and across her taut belly. Nothing. I tried manipulating the small instrument back and forth, in a circle, up and down, as if it were a searchlight in a dark room, and I used the connect-the-dots map for the likely locations of the fetuses. Nothing.

And then, suddenly, I caught one: galloping hooves, a frantic, fast-paced *clippety-clop*. No *whoosh-whoosh*, or *lub-dub*, *lub-dub*, like in humans, but a quick, multitoned beat, so fast it was hard to count the pulses. I pressed the Doppler head in even deeper, and the sound magnified. There was no doubt that I had found a puppy. Here was 200, then 210, then 225— the desired rate.

By the time I was done and ready to go to bed, I had heard six and accordingly marked the spots where they were on her belly with a green felt-tip Sharpie, as recommended, to help me locate them the next day and afterward. Brad and I joked that now she was a black-and-white-and-green spotted dog. Before I finished up that night, I went back to the first heartbeat, the one I could hear most clearly, just to listen one more time. And there it was, galloping onward to sweet dreams.

nineteen

TWO WEEKS BEFORE BREEZE'S due date, while Dawn was gone on a two-week vacation and I was still waiting for the next X-ray, I sat on the bed beside her and slid the uterine monitor under her belly. I had just gotten off the phone with Myrna, who was feeling poorly. The temperature was in the 90s, with only a little breeze that fluttered at the curtain over the window.

Breeze didn't complain, so neither did I. I felt as if we were a team, like a mother and daughter who were going to Lamaze classes together. She stretched out on her side, let me slide the monitoring disk under her (with Karen's approval, we had abandoned the straps and tether method), and then wagged her tail. Because she wasn't allowed to move at all, I had devised a system to keep her from moving her tail as well: a pillow kept that metronome of happiness still.

As these sessions had become more routine, Breeze had likewise become more relaxed about them. Despite being an active, rambunctious Dal who liked to play with her blue football more than she liked to eat (well, almost), she seemed to sense the need to do these exercises, and so held still for the entire hour without moving even a bit, other than that enthusiastic tail. She just closed her eyes and took a long snooze.

This afternoon, as usual, after we were finished and she had been joyfully released from her position of immobility, I sent the recording in to the base station.

The phone rang quickly. "She's in labor," Karen said, "and it's too early by twelve days."

Panic set in. My adrenaline began to surge. "What do we do?" Never had I been so glad to say "we."

"Get on the phone to the vet and get her some terbutaline and some progesterone. Tell them it's an emergency."

A quick call to Dr. Cain's office informed me that she was away in Italy for the month, so I called our regular animal hospital, only to be told that Dr. Dickley was in surgery. I pressed his technician to go and ask for the prescription, but when she did, Dr. Dickley sent back word that he never prescribed either drug, that Breeze was aborting the litter and nothing could be done. "He says you can deliver her at home," the tech reported. "Or if you feel you can't handle a stillborn litter, you can bring her in here and we'll take care of it for you."

I hung up with a bang. Obviously, there was a solution— Karen's solution. As midwife to litter after litter, she had handled many that were premature. And even I recognized terbutaline from my days, back in the eighties, with my high-risk pregnancy with Nathaniel. Terbutaline was hardly a novel drug. I was not going to find any answers for Breeze's predicament with Dr. Dickley, whom I now perceived as downright ignorant.

I quickly dialed Dr. Cain's office again, looking for some help from someone there, anyone, but was told, sympathetically, that there was no one covering her reproductive patients.

And so I began frantically combing the Bay Area for a vet who knew about terbutaline and would prescribe it.

Dawn was still on vacation. Alone with my fear, I would not surrender to sitting there helplessly. Yet, everywhere I turned, knowledgeable vets were away for weeks or were over a four-hour drive from my home. I called WhelpWise once more, and this time Karen suggested that I call Dr. Cain's service back one more time and ask to speak with her technician. Maybe she would be able to introduce me to someone else on staff who would be willing to work with WhelpWise, even if they had no prior experience with the team there.

Over the phone I met Dr. Bain (an odd but auspicious name twist), who had heard of terbutaline and progesterone injections to stop canine labor and told me to come in immediately.

I took off for the office over the long San Mateo Bridge, driving as safely past the speed limit as I thought prudent, but still I was terrified that Breeze would give birth in the car, as the office was an hour away. When I got there, I was rewarded by a genuinely gratifying experience: Dr. Bain had no ego problem with letting WhelpWise chart the course we would follow. My anxiety began to ease a bit. Suddenly we were in compassionate and knowledgeable hands.

But a quick X-ray, still earlier than the one we had scheduled with Dr. Dickley, was imperative now to predict the puppies' development, and it revealed only some slight skeletal improvement. It wasn't what we needed or wanted to see because it meant they weren't developed enough to be born. We were at least twelve days away from a normal delivery, which in a human birth would mean only that the prospective baby needed a stay in a neonatal intensive care unit, but which for a dog meant the death of the pups because a dog's gestational period was so much shorter—sixty-three days rather than nine months.

And even then, the situation was more complicated than I had first understood. Progesterone played a large part in the premature labor, and so Dr. Bain was reluctant to administer the terbutaline immediately, without testing her blood levels; for complicated reasons, if the progesterone should still be normal, the terbutaline would have little or no effect and do nothing toward stopping the labor.

I didn't want to wait. "Is there some side effect to the terbutaline that could endanger her or the pups?" I asked quietly.

"No, but it might just be a waste of time and money until we know the blood levels."

I shook my head. "But I don't care about those. If we give the terbutaline now, we won't have lost anything, whereas if we wait and the levels *are* low, she will probably go into hard labor soon, and by tomorrow afternoon when the test comes in, it'll be too late."

He tapped his teeth with his pen and paused for a minute. Then he pulled out his prescription pad.

The tech did a blood draw marked urgent. Still, the results wouldn't come back until late the following afternoon.

Back at home I texted Dawn. I called Michele, who was extremely concerned and sympathetic; Breeze was part of her family, too. She remarked that it must be hard to have Dawn away at this particular time. Vehemently, I agreed. Dawn called quite quickly to check on Breeze's progress, but how I wished she were here to help keep this particular vigil. The time the puppies required to remain in utero stretched out like a long solitary road before me.

The next morning, a call came from Dr. Bain, who indicated

that the progesterone was indeed low. What a good thing it was that I had a vet who would work with me instead of ignoring me. Being pushy had paid off.

The next twelve days went by: one hour, then the next. The medication had to be administered every eight hours exactly, preceded by a monitoring session of an hour's duration so that we could assess whether we needed to increase the dose. Breeze lay on her side, eyes closed, the very essence of patience. Sometimes, on the 5:00 AM shift, we would doze together, the green light of the recorder blinking, just perceptible through my half-mast eyes. Gone were the days of frolicking in the yard: she was allowed no exercise and had to be walked on a leash.

Each time I waited for the report to come in, I felt I was clinging to a cliff: she would have two or three contractions in the hour with high uterine irritability; then the next session, there would be no contractions with no irritability. Back and forth it went. We were picking our way through a minefield, waiting every eight hours for the news I feared the most—the word that hard labor had started and could not be stopped. And always, after each session, Breeze rolled onto her back so that I could spend another forty-five minutes measuring the magical heartbeats that galloped away beneath the thin wall of her skin, just under my fingertips. The puppies began to poke back at me with their paws, their legs, butting their heads against the pressure of the Doppler. I didn't need an X-ray to tell me they had bones now.

The final day of waiting drew near. I began to believe we would make it, that my wish for a healthy litter would be fulfilled, that a boy would come into my life again. Anxiety began to give way to hope.

PART IX

the puppy pen

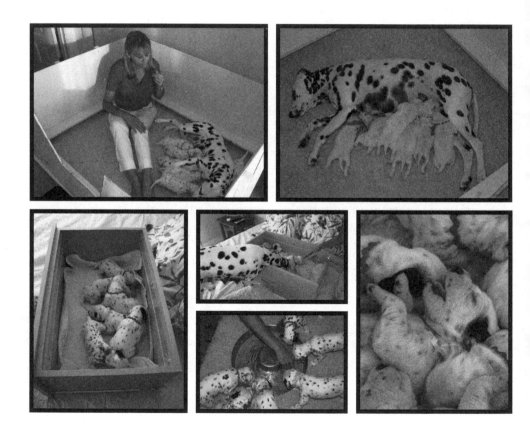

{NOT IN ORDER OF APPEARANCE}

Pink

Blue

Purple

Green

Red

Yellow

twenty

WHELPWISE HAD ADVISED US that because the first shot of progesterone had stilled the uterus for so long, the uterus might not respond well to the rigors of labor. The pups could be at risk, and so Dawn and I had grown resigned to the idea that Breeze must have an elective Cesarean section. Dawn came home at last, and on Sunday night, July 10, Dr. Cain returned from Italy and called us immediately after she saw the reports that had come in during her absence. We were to bring Breeze in first thing in the morning so that she could see how my girl was doing.

After I spoke with Dr. Cain, Brad helped me out by doing the monitoring session himself while I went to bed early. He was given the all clear by WhelpWise and woke me to say so. No contractions at all. I got up to check her and give her a hug on my way to the bathroom and thought that she was acting a bit on the strange side. She had moved from her regular bed on the chair to the one Gulliver had used once he couldn't jump up onto his chair, now tucked away in the corner. I had never been able to bring myself to put it away. Restlessly she turned around and around on its cushions, circling. It looked like early labor to me, but WhelpWise had told Brad things were copacetic.

I woke him to ask if he was sure that the sensor had been well enough tucked under her body. At his sleepy nod, I went back to bed and promised myself I'd check her again in an hour.

But it wasn't till the alarm went off at five o'clock that I woke. I got up to do the early-morning session and sent the report in over the modem at six. A few minutes later, Karen called: Breeze was in active labor. She called Dr. Cain for me while I got everything ready for our trip across the bay.

While Dawn was driving up from her house, I packed the car like a whelping box, just in case Breeze delivered en route. Sheets, towels, the warming box, and a microwave disk, shaped like a solid Frisbee, which would help keep the pups warm after they were born. Everything went into a suitcase and the suitcase went into the car and Dawn and I took off for San Ramon.

As soon as we arrived, they monitored her and reported back that she was indeed in hard labor. A C-section was quickly set up, and before we knew it, we were standing in front of a large glass window watching the surgery. Dr. Cain made a long incision along the abdomen and then began reaching inside. Out came one of the long uterine "horns" where the puppies still nested, attached by their umbilical cords. I felt faint, as I had initially with Rhiannon's whelping, knelt on the floor for a minute, and then stood again, determined not to miss the unfolding scene.

Dr. Cain was tugging so hard that the muscles in her arms stood out in sharp relief. One by one, she began to pull them out. It was like extracting a wine cork from a bottle. Later she would tell us that one of the pups had been wedged into the birth canal, undoubtedly causing the irritable action of the uterus over the last two weeks, and because he was blocking the exit, none of them would have survived a natural whelping.

As we watched, out popped the first head. An assembly line of techs waited with their hands out, ready to get each pup going. They shook the mucus and fluid from the puppies' lungs, then warmed them with a brisk rubdown, handling them as roughly as the mother would have until we heard that first magical cry, just a small peep into the world.

But one of the things every Dal breeder doesn't want to see was apparent as that first babe slid out into the world: a patch, dark black, marring the smooth pink color of the ear. A patch was an instant disqualification for the show ring, though puppies so marked made wonderful pets and were often the first sold out of a litter because of the dramatic asymmetrical marking. We bit back our disappointment and kept peering into the surgical suite as the rest made their entrance into the world. Number two and three and four and five and six arrived, all healthy, all mewling and squirming with life.

But by the time Dr. Cain was closing the incision with strong sutures, it was obvious that one girl and two boys out of the six were patched. My main emotion was one of relief at this living litter, one that we had so nearly lost. Still, 50 percent of them were patched. I comforted myself that at least there still was the chance of a show boy for me.

We were given a thermal box lined with a heating pad for the small white infants, who had no spots at all except for the three with their inky patches. They climbed over each other, mewing like kittens, reminding me of those early days at home when Rosie and Violet gave birth. When we switched the pups to the warming box I had brought with me, so carefully prepared, it was hilariously too small, and the newborns immediately began a concerted escape routine, though they were both blind and weak. Up they went and down we pushed, gently.

I looked eagerly for the boy who was destined to be mine. I found him and scooped him up with care. That was when I saw it: an under-ear patch, small but definite. I was dumbfounded. There was no show boy here for me after all. The litter was 80 percent patched.

How could this have happened? Bad luck, perhaps, or something we, as breeders, just didn't understand yet. It was all part of the crapshoot, the uncertainty of what you could get: the litter could be all girls and no boys, patches, deafs, no show puppies at all. Stupidly, I hadn't prepared myself for such an outcome. I hadn't said to myself, there may be no puppy here for me. I had just listened to those heartbeats joyfully, waiting for my boy to be born, waiting for another boy whom I could love in some of the ways I had loved Gulliver.

I had hoped to curl up with him in the evening on my bed, to whisper in his ear, to have his soft eyes regard me with patience and love. And to pick up where I had left off: bonding with him as we raced around the show ring. I had wanted to launch Literati once again. In this instant, that became an impossibility. Dawn would take her pick of the girls, and there was only a very slim chance that both would be show quality and that one could be mine. And only if, I cautioned myself, I had wanted to keep a female, and have two bitches in my household, after all my troubled history with Rhiannon and Tia.

No boy for me repeated like a mantra in my mind. It seemed a bitter turn of circumstance that there were two girls for Dawn to choose from and nothing for me to keep. I was envious while she was cheerful; though of course there were many hurdles yet to cross, she nevertheless had a shot at finding the little girl she wanted.

As I drove home, I tried simply to listen to the little cries I could hear from the backseat, where Dawn sat with the cardboard box on her lap. I unpacked the car and drew the towel on the top of the box aside so that Brad could have a peek. I looked down at them and felt, despite my disappointment, like a proud parent, and I could tell from Brad's face that he felt the same. For him, it didn't matter a bit whether there was a show puppy. And while it did matter to me, it mattered more that they were all alive.

We carried the babies into the house and helped Breeze out of the car, mindful of her stitches and her ordeal. And then we settled everyone in to the new nursery.

twenty-one

THE VET HAD WARNED us that after a C-Section, Breeze might have a difficult time accepting her pups. We wouldn't be able to leave her alone with them for even a minute. And so I sat for hours in the whelping box with her, keeping my hand on her head so that there was no chance of her snapping and maiming one of the babies, or of cannibalization—all grim possibilities for a bitch who had not seen her whelp be born, who had looked down at them for the first time and wondered, *What the hell are these?*

Nevertheless, when I put the puppies on her teats, Breeze let them nurse avidly even though she looked somewhat mystified as they sought the colostrum she had to offer until her milk came in, their little paws vigorously kneading and growing a bit bloody from her incision. Now they cried not at all. Just suckle, suckle, suckle. She growled only once.

Dawn spent the first night to help me, but by the second day, she had to go to work, and I was on my own. I began picking them up, and they felt good in my hands, the skin on their bodies like—as breeders are wont to say—a snugly fitting glove. The green pup looked a little skinny, so I put him on the rear teats first, where extra milk would eventually come in. I checked them at night in their cardboard box, as I slept only a bit, in a broken fashion. Breeze stayed in her whelping box, and I adjusted the heat lamp if she seemed too hot, but it had to be warm enough that I could settle them in with her every hour or so to nurse.

By the third day, she was as comfortable with them as if her pregnancy, labor, and delivery had been totally natural, and I was able to relinquish my role as guard. She became a very attentive mother. Quickly, a new nickname was bestowed: "Big Mama," even though, of course, she had always been so petite. Her milk was late due to the medications we had given her preterm, and so I tried to supplement the puppies. While Brad sat sentry duty, I went to four stores looking for more of the recommended goats' milk puppy formula and infant-size nipples and bottles. The one jar I'd bought previously was woefully inadequate. Or so I thought. Once I got it all home, I realized it was concentrated and that I had enough for a canine army. In any case, they spit it out and cried piteously.

The other problem was that she was refusing to truly clean them. A mother dog stimulates the urination and defecation of the pups by licking them with her tongue until they pee or poop, and then she eats it right up. To a breeder it is a welcome sign—as otherwise you have to take a warm moist cotton ball and wipe and wipe. And wipe.

It takes forever to elicit poop from that tiny opening using a cotton ball, and so I was up at night after each feeding, wiping, with sleep in my eyes, cursing at Breeze. For three days, I was at it every two hours, which was about how often they fed. I'd just finish with the last pup and then have to start over again with the first. It reminded me of breastfeeding Nathaniel and

Gabe when they were infants—an endless treadmill of effort. The lack of rest caught up with me late that first week, and on July 21, my fifty-eighth birthday, the doctor informed me I had double pneumonia. I discovered I really didn't care. Where in another time of my life I might have gone to bed and moaned, at this point, I only took the antibiotics and stayed on my feet: puppies wait for nothing and no one—not even a sick surrogate parent. And so I kept giving them the best care I could: handling them over and over, changing their sheepskin pads, weighing them, changing their rickrack, and feeding Breeze four times a day while making sure she was doing her various jobs as a mother. And when she didn't lick, lick, lick, I wiped, wiped, wiped.

I tried to sleep at night but often found myself just sitting in the puppy pen under the glow of the ceramic heat lamp, my bottom getting wet from tiny pee spots on the sheepskin as I held the little ones in my lap. I was still amazed at their survival. Watching Breeze sleep curled around the nest of her offspring, I remembered the way she had lain on the bed on the other side of this very room while I measured the frequency of contractions during her preterm labor.

During those late nights or early morning hours, it seemed to me that sometimes things do work out the way they are meant to—though usually when I said this to myself, I was trying to rationalize something emotionally difficult or painful. I had repeated it time and time again after losing Gulliver, not understanding the sense of his death, but trying to find peace in the idea that someday I would understand why he had been taken from me. Now, fourteen months after his passing, as I sat amid the life in my puppy box, I reminded myself that the old adage applied in a positive way. This time I had gotten lucky. My babies had been born alive. The patches seemed to matter less.

By day five, the puppies had taken hold of the teats tightly enough that I didn't have to keep them there, and Breeze's milk began to flow. She didn't produce copiously, but it was enough. Slowly, the pups began to gain weight, with Yellow being the hog of the box. He nursed fast and then pushed the others out of the way to find another spot. All of them yelped and struggled to find the little teats they couldn't see and cried when I held them in my hand or cuddled them. I had forgotten that they wanted only to be with Mommy during this stage. I had forgotten so much—but the situation demanded that I remember again, and quickly. Dawn came by two or three times a week to help with some of the work, but it was my name that would precede hers as breeder on the puppies' registration certificates, so my greater effort was only fair. Michele called weekly, checking on their progress, and we had the chance to get to know one another even better. When they were a few weeks old, she came to visit and pronounced them a lovely litter.

Myrna, however, who had listened so faithfully throughout Breeze's pregnancy, had withdrawn into her illness as her symptoms now worsened, and though we made several dates for her to come and visit, she fell ill before each one. I called her every night to report the progress of the pups—continuing to try to distract her with news of the outside world—and invited her up to visit, but I saw at last that she just wasn't strong enough to make the twenty-minute drive. It looked as if another surgery was imminent, imperative to reduce the size of the growing tumor. I could no longer set aside my worry for her. Maybe somehow she would survive, just the way my babies had, but for the first time, I had begun to question my own sense of hope.

. . .

During that first week, they were little white piglets that did nothing but squirm onto their mother's teats and then tumble off into a puppy pile to keep warm. Nothing but eat and sleep and cry. They looked unbelievably fragile. One thing I remembered for sure: handling them as infants was as important as making sure they were nursing sufficiently. And so I did, nonstop.

At two weeks, they weighed almost three times what they had at birth. When their color came in, they turned into a spotted band of blind and deaf little beings, crawling on weak legs around their whelping box. At day fourteen, I noticed that their eyes had started to open, just a tiny crack at first, beginning on the lid at the side nearest the nose and then slowly, over the next few days, opening outward until a tiny blue orb was visible.

It would be a little while longer before their eye color turned the normal Dalmatian brown, *if* it did. There was always the chance of some blue eyes in the litter, even though this was not preferable in a show dog—but it would not be a disqualification, like a patch. I could see that nose and eye trim would fill, so we didn't have to worry about that. I kept my fingers crossed that the two girls who weren't patched would have nice dark brown eyes and, most important, would not be deaf.

I knew they could see only big, blurry shapes, but I persisted in holding them up to my face and whispering to them even though their tiny earflaps were still sealed. I figured it couldn't hurt. I figured I needed it for myself. Boys or girls, patched or not, they all needed me. And I needed them.

I didn't let myself think about whether or not they heard the world around them. Maybe they could feel the vibrations of my voice. Maybe the warmth of my hands and cheeks was comforting in their brave new world. In the meantime, they kept stumbling around the pen and banging their heads into the sides. I would have to wait another ten days or so before they could track a moving ball, or really differentiate my face from its surroundings. By the third week, they were lurching around on trembling legs like little drunken sailors. And hearing was suddenly a big issue—but it was one I didn't want to worry about. So, uncharacteristically, I didn't.

Both Nathaniel and Gabe stopped by intermittently, drawn by their interest in the rapidly growing puppies, more interested in visiting with them than with me. Which was fine. Over time, I simply needed all the hands I could get on the pups to socialize them. And so later, once it was safe, I welcomed each person who wanted to come and visit, no matter how inconvenient the timing, and filled in the puppies' social calendar as fully as I could. I even imported neighborhood children I didn't know for the cause.

One by one, I took them out of the whelping box for the first time and set them down, gently, on the floor. They cruised around the guest room. Soon I was laughing at their early attempts at investigation. Purple was a scent hound and followed her nose everywhere, getting stuck under the bed. Yellow was cautious, but thorough, winding up with a dust kitten in his mouth. Red was an explorer, examining everything I would allow him to reach, putting his face in the water dish—which I had begun leaving out even though they had yet to drink anything—and blowing great big bubbles through his nose. Green was shy, uncertain, and would only cuddle up by my side. Pink was confident, off and running as soon as I set her on the rug, and I had to watch her to make sure she wouldn't get into the electrical cords under the side table. Blue was sleepy to start, sitting down and yawning as if unimpressed by this big new world, and then coming over to nose my hand enthusiastically.

Week four was marked by Breeze's resistance to feeding them. Their sharp, needlelike teeth had mostly broken through their gums, and though I worried that maybe they weren't getting enough milk, they were certainly fat and sassy. Now there was a lot of lip-smacking while they nursed, as they stripped the milk down with expert suction. It didn't take long before the first teat was empty, and on instinct, it seemed, they began pushing each other around, fiercely hunting down one that was still full. Instinct, I thought, an instinct that lets them thrive even though one of their brothers might go hungry.

It was time to wean them and move them upstairs, out to the larger pen in the garage, where there was one area for their sheepskin rug and another with newspaper pellets for peeing and pooping. Dogs don't like to soil the area where they sleep, so they would box-train themselves and make cleanup easier for me. This would eventually help potty and crate-train them, as they grew old enough to be more independent and ready for their new homes. The idea of those new homes weighed on me with every week that passed. Our time together was so short. It was halfway over.

Now, when Breeze finished her cursory nursing and cleaned up the box, she would run quickly to join us in the kitchen. She was ready to be a housedog again and to leave mothering behind. At first I was dismayed. What kind of a mother was she? But then I understood better: her babies were like teenagers—soon she would shoo them from the nest she had made for them, into the outside world. And I, in the meantime, took on the role of full-time mother: I would clean the pen, bring the food, and play with them in the outdoor run.

On the fourth Saturday, Brad and I made the trek to the garage, each with a puppy in our arms, over the stairs three times. We had set up the larger weaning pen there so that they would have more space to move around in. Once set down in their new home, the puppies explored their big new surroundings from corner to corner, slipping and sliding on the pellets, but after a while settled down to sleep in exhaustion. The next day, for their first real meal, I ground up premium puppy chow in the blender with water to make a thin gruel, then put it into the round stainless steel pan that looked like a flying saucer. It had an elevated middle bump and an open track around the circumference to help them avoid stepping in the food as they learned to eat it.

I had been certain they wouldn't even go near it, but they enthusiastically chowed down and put their front paws in to get better purchase for lapping it up. Soon they were covered in brown goo, and this time, Breeze was happy to get into the pen and lick them clean. Soon the yellow puppy became the champion of the puppy pan. We were still calling him the hog of the box, as I had to hold him aloft till the others got their fill and then set him back down to gulp whatever was left.

Suddenly, we hit the five-week marker, and they were crawling up and out of the pen and landing on the other side with a resounding thump. Brad built new and higher sides.

A few days later, we raised the sides of the pen once again, so that now it looked like the Great Wall of China, and we marveled for yet another time how quickly they were growing. My stomach tightened each time Brad commented on it. They were only five weeks old and yet had begun the task of challenging themselves in their life—even if this only meant contesting the height of the walls that penned them in. There were only three weeks left.

They mouthed the toys and each other constantly. There were real toys in the pen now, like cow's hooves, and a rubber ball, three Nylabones, and two sets of plastic keys. Anything that was good against which to grind their teeth. Their hearing looked good, but when other people, or Dawn, asked what I was thinking on that score, I still refused to commit myself, and I didn't walk around whistling and clapping my hands, either.

I remembered the mistakes I had made with Rhiannon's litter and had instructed myself to be more patient. It did seem that they all raised their heads and came running in a black-and-white tide when I brought over their supper and breakfast pans, calling out the high-pitched sing-song "Pup pup pup puppppy!" Nevertheless, I remained resolutely quiet on the subject. I would wait for the BAER hearing test that would be administered in our home at the beginning of the next week.

Corinne was an audiologist who worked at UC Davis doing the specialized test, and she went on the road a few days a week with her equipment. She arrived with her computer and her probes on a Tuesday morning. I had awakened early that day, just as the summer light was coming in around the shades in our bedroom. I hadn't wanted this day to come, remembering little Purple from Ashley's litter and how Pat had fainted at the vet's office after we'd put the puppy to sleep. Thinking about Pat—and then, inevitably, Myrna—had made me sad, but I had shaken it off, fed the pups, and poured myself a cup of coffee. There was a lot to do on this sunny August morning.

One by one, Corinne and Dawn and I set each puppy on a towel on the top of my kitchen counter, and she inserted the tiny probes behind the neck, pushed the rubber sensor deep into the ear, and turned on the machine. Dawn and I watched the graph needle going up and down as it traced a spidery gray line. The puppies' lives depended on that line. If it were flat, then I would have to face the terrible task ahead of me. I knew nothing more about saving and training deaf dogs than I had fourteen years before, when Ashley's litter was born.

As we progressed from one pup to the next, double-checking each result with a second test, it became obvious that all of them could hear. As I ferried them back and forth to their pen, anxiety on the way in, relief on the way back, I kissed them on their necks and blessed them one by one. I would not have to euthanize anyone this time around. I thought of Me-Me, walking around the kitchen as the puppies surged around her ankles, banging her wooden spoon against a pot to see if they all alerted to the noise. I wondered what my parents would have done if there had been a deaf. Would it have been sent to the farm, real or imagined?

It is only now, seven months after the litter was born, that I at last begin to hear of trainers who work with deafs. Now there are some breeders who send any temperamentally reliable deaf to be so trained. It appears that, with hand signals, many deaf pups can become lovable house pets, or sometimes, even obedience or agility dogs. They glue themselves to the side of their owners in an unusual way. With such rapt and consistent attention, they are able to work successfully, and they are trained from the outset to have their owner constantly in their sightline. While they cannot run free, without a leash, it sounds like a fine trade-off to me, but I will release a deaf only to someone who specializes in training them. Many of them live with Dals and other breeds who cannot hear, and many of them have successfully placed deafs into pet homes.

Unfortunately, when Breeze's puppies were born, the ethical guidelines for DCA (whose guidelines I had signed when

I joined) still held that all deaf pups should be euthanized early in life, and breeders were sharply, and painfully, divided about which direction to choose. Those who favored euthanization—to err on the safe side—were horrified by and angry with those who favored training. The latter, who believed in training—to err on the compassionate side—were horrified by and angry with the former. Those who favored euthanization had arguments like "a deaf dog will run out into the street and be hit by a car," or "deaf dogs turn and snap when startled." The latter had arguments like "*any* dog can run out into the street and be hit by a car; no dog should be off leash near a road," and "the startle reflex in deaf dogs can be conquered with a particular kind of work."

It was a no-win situation, and I thanked God I wouldn't have to deal with it until my next litter. In the meanwhile, I struck up a correspondence with a therapy dog trainer who worked not only with hearing dogs but also with "deafies," as she referred to them, and her calling in life intrigued me. She gave me advice on training the average dog, her emails filled with tips and tidbits. Now that I was on the online groups ShowDals and DCA Members—the Dal breeders' lists that discussed everything from who had won at Westminster, to how to best microchip your own dog, to the quandary of deaf puppies—I was more a part of the Dal family than ever before. Eventually she would fly to California for three days, and I would drive her a long distance to rescue a deaf puppy whose breeder had decided to surrender, rather than to euthanize. Yet, I would tell no one what I had done, except Brad and my kids. The move to save deafies was for the most part still secret, an underground railroad of sorts.

· · ·

It was time for my pups to meet the outside world. They were current on their shots and had been wormed twice by then, so it was relatively safe to expose them to others and others to them. They still couldn't travel anywhere and be set down, as there were too many viruses waiting to be picked up from people's or other dogs' feet, but it was safe to have outside visitors in our home with certain precautions taken.

I called Myrna again, even though I knew there was little chance of her coming. We both knew, and didn't say, that this was probably the last opportunity she would have to visit them. The pups had taken over my life for the last five weeks, and we had been relegated to phone call visits because I couldn't really get away for long periods of time to drive her to chemo sessions or PET scans, which sometimes could last six hours or more. Her voice was growing progressively weaker, and often I had to strain to hear her. I gave up on the idea that she would ever see the puppies before they went to their new homes. Her condition had gone so rapidly downhill that I couldn't keep up with it. She was still driving, but I wondered for how much longer she would be able to do that.

Without being told, she knew how much I wanted her to meet them. And so one afternoon she did manage to come up, insisting on bringing herself rather than allowing me to come down and collect her and then take her home again. She said she was feeling stronger. We hadn't seen each other since Breeze's premature labor had begun. She was too sick to even think about having lunch and really didn't want to eat anyway. She had lost a great deal of weight.

Now that the puppies were older, I had vowed to start driving to her medical appointments again, and shortly after our visit with the pups, I did. But when I saw her that day I was even more worried: how drawn and frail she looked. It moved me that she wanted to share something so important to me, despite her illness. She had never gotten to know Breeze the way she had Gully, and so she felt at a greater remove than she would have had these been Gully's pups. Nevertheless, when she held them in her arms, they brought life into her lap. Without really realizing it, I unconsciously accepted that she would probably never make this trip again.

• • •

Dawn and I began to set up appointment times with prospective buyers. They were eager to come and see the puppies, but I felt as ferocious as a mama bear when they arrived on my doorstep. Once in the door, visitors had to remove their shoes and wash their hands against possible infection. Lest I seem too paranoid, I told them many breeders make you step in solutions doctored with chlorine bleach to guard against parvovirus. Maybe I seemed weird, but frankly, I didn't care. It was all part of my job.

I handed the puppies over one by one, showing the children in the families how to hold them safely. I hovered, counseling everyone to sit so that they couldn't be dropped from a standing height. The pups squirmed to be set down and then romped around the pen, showing off. But slowly, one by one, they came and climbed up on the strangers' laps, curious, ready now to welcome these new people and lick their faces. They were cute, cute, cute, and everyone wanted to take more than one home with them. But I wouldn't sell two to anyone, believing that if a buyer took home more than one, brother and sister would bond with each other, rather than with the family.

Everyone wanted to pick out his or her own puppy, but Dawn and I began steering certain people in particular directions, according to our experience. It seemed wiser to put a female into a home where there was a male, and vice versa, in order to avoid future dominance issues among same-sex dogs. In houses with small children, we preferred to place the most self-assured, secure dogs and not one who appeared, even at this point, shy or standoffish. A big barreling dog like Yellow wouldn't work well in a home with an elderly couple; he needed a place where he would get a lot of exercise, maybe with teenagers. And so we counseled prospective families: "Don't get your heart set on a certain pup. Remember that we've got to see how the temperaments develop." The temperament testing wouldn't be done until the seventh week, and then we would learn more about who should go where. But it was hard to hold these eager people off.

At six weeks, some of the people were just coming back for a second look. "Which one, which one?" they clamored.

"We like red!"

"We want yellow."

I didn't say a word. I didn't say that I already had made my mind up that Red, my young explorer, was going to live with a couple up in Oregon who were looking for a pup who would make a good search-and-rescue dog. They had trained many SAR dogs before and had told me the traits they were looking for in a pup. I was excited at the prospect of having a puppy who was going to be working in this field, and I was sure I had the right one for them: Red was the one who got his nose right to the ground the first time out of the whelping pen on the rug in the guest room. I was already certain that he was going to make a fine working dog.

When Barb and Kurt made the long trip down in their truck to meet the pups, and I opened the door into the garage, Red ran from the puppy pile where he had been napping, straight to the wall of the pen to investigate the newcomers. As Kurt bent over to say hello, Red jumped up in his face and began to lick him as vigorously as only a puppy can. This extroverted friendliness was sheer Red—curious, investigative—but Barb and Kurt didn't know that. To them it looked like a sign from above. And maybe it was. But in any case, I knew I had made my match.

. . .

In the seventh week we faced the Volhard temperament test, which would give us the final word on who would go where, although I had already pretty much made up my mind about this, all the while counting the wishes of the prospective owners into the equation as well. The results would help predict the temperament of each pup as he grew older and the kind of dog he would grow up to be—but it would probably not give me any information I didn't already have. I knew them as I knew my own children. Nevertheless, the test was a good secondary measure, and just about all Dalmatian breeders did it on their litters. It was common in other breeds as well.

One at a time, each puppy was put into a tall, sheet-clad pen—in our bedroom—so that he couldn't look out, and where he had never been before so that it couldn't smell familiar. Then he had to face a total stranger, in this case, Marty Stanford, the breeder from my young beginnings in Dals and with whom I had remained casual friends throughout the years. She would put them through a series of exercises.

First off, the pup was set on the ground and called by the tester. If he did not come readily, it was interpreted as a sign of shyness. The others were similar, simple actions that measured the pup's response. The series of ten included a retrieve with a paper ball, a startle reflex test with an umbrella that opened suddenly in their faces, a "follow" to see how sociable they were, a toe pinch to determine how much physical correction they would need during training, a cuddle following that pinch to see how forgiving they were.

By the time we were done, I was not surprised with a single result. Purple was independent, Yellow was still bossy, Blue was confident, Pink was active, Red explored confidently, and Green was as shy as ever. They were all mine, and I knew them in ways no one else did, not Brad, not Dawn.

Two weeks before, we had at last named them: it was famous people this time, despite various votes for baseball players or notable sports figures (Nathaniel's and Brad's suggestions). But I did something different instead. Pink was sassy, so I named her Marilyn (Monroe) but Brad called her Pinkerbelle. That sassy attitude would carry her far. When she went to live with Dawn, as first female pick of the litter, she was renamed Adele, after the singer, and went on to become a renowned Grand Champion, surpassing even her mother's record and winning the prestigious class of Futurity, as well as Sweepstakes and Reserve Winner's Bitch at her first National. The following year she went Best of Opposite Sex to the number one Dal in the country. Adele would develop as my first truly major homebred dog, as Dawn took her well up in the standings of the Top Twenty Dalmatians in the country.

Yellow got to be J.W., after John Wayne, because he was the macho boss of the puppy box. Purple was Audrey (Hepburn) because of her classy attitude. Blue had two extraordinary deep blue eyes, so she was Elizabeth Taylor, or Lizzie. And Red, my adventurer since day one, who believed that nothing could stop him, was named by Brad: Lewis, after Meriwether Lewis from the

Lewis and Clark Expedition. Green got Green Bean—an oddball name, created by me just because it rhymed, the kind of nonsensical nickname I'd given the dogs in the past. Almost none of the names stuck—only Green Bean whose owners kept it. Go figure.

They were pretty big now, weighing in at about ten pounds. Their play had grown aggressive, as they discovered how hard they could bite without causing, or receiving, pain. They were acquiring all the skills they would need when they left me. It was only two weeks away, and my life still revolved around them. I was doing no work. I was seeing few friends. I had allowed them to take over my life.

Myrna's condition was rapidly worsening. Perhaps I hid my face behind those of my puppies. I didn't want to lose any of them.

. . .

It was so very close to the time when they would go, and I already knew that I would hold on to them as tightly as if they were my own children before I put them into their new mothers' and fathers' arms; I knew I would cry myself dry-eyed once I had shut the kitchen door and had some privacy. Public tears would be more than embarrassing because a breeder was supposed to be immune to the vibrancy of such emotions, more used to such comings and goings, but I knew that the puppies' departures would stay with me for quite a while.

Because Breeze had weaned the pups at four weeks, she was no longer invested in them. She spent most of her time in the house with us and ran in to check on them only occasionally. When they left, she would not exhibit any signs of loss or depression.

However, it was different for me. The transition of these bumptious pups out of my life would bring the specter of loss back in, a reversal of the way their birth had brought joy to my life seven weeks before. I would have to relinquish those whom I had loved so intensely, and would continue to love, no matter where they lived, just as I had relinquished into memory the lives of family and friends who were now gone. All these young ones cuddled and kissed my face, in their own way. All played rough-and-tumble and cried when hurt, or at being left alone, or waiting to be fed, in a manner particular to them. They were most certainly blessed with their own characters, and I mourned them that way, each unto his own. They would never be far from my mind once they were gone. And I would keep tabs on them by following up with their new owners.

But gone they would be, and how I would hate that. I had experienced so many other losses of love: my father's sister Joan, to whom I was so close, in a drunk-driving accident, when I was sixteen; my mother to suicide, when I was twenty-one; my Nana to stroke, when I was thirty-four; Melanie, the first of my own peer group, to breast cancer, when I was forty-six; Rose to lung cancer, when I was forty-seven; Pat to colon cancer, when I was fifty-four; Diane to a rare brain cancer, when I was fifty-five; and last but hardly least, my adored Gulliver, when I was fifty-seven, two years back—the death I still mourned the most.

It reminded me of a symphony, with its echoing themes, and it accumulated power as it accelerated toward whatever the next moment would bring. I now accepted that Myrna was on the crest of the wave that was carrying her, inexorably, to the end. Suffering terrible and prolonged pain, she would at last be swept under by a tide beyond anyone's control.

going home

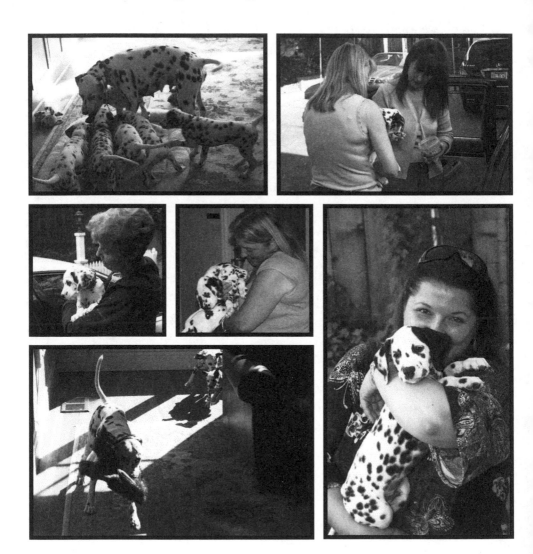

{IN ORDER OF DISAPPEARANCE}

Purple, a.k.a. Darcy

Red, a.k.a. Riley

Blue, a.k.a. Izzy

Pink, a.k.a. Adele

Green, a.k.a. Green Bean

Yellow, a.k.a. Cody

twenty-two

AND THEN, AS SUDDENLY as the old month blew out, the new month blew in. September had arrived. The puppies were jumping and climbing all over me as I sat in the dog run trying to write on one long, hot afternoon just before they went to their new homes. They were now eight weeks old. Red attacked my feet; Yellow raced around and jumped on everyone until they rolled onto their backs in submission. Then he got distracted and came over to paw at my lined pad of paper and tried to make off with the pen. Once again, I was trying my hand at a book—this book, begun that day in the puppy pen.

Green Bean pulled on the drawstrings of my capri pants until they unlaced, and then he climbed into my lap to try to get into his favorite position of curling around my neck like a cat, before I pushed him off. Purple bumped against my butt where it pressed against the bottom of the camp chair. Blue scratched her back and then bounced across my sneaker. Only Pink had peacefully subsided into the other chair, and I remembered how, last week, when I came into the garage one morning with the breakfast pan, she was sitting up pretty on the floor, having managed to scale even the highest wall of the puppy pen. It was so tall now that I had to climb on a ladder to get in to clean the pen and change the pad.

I gave up on writing, put my face up into the sun, and thought about the bond I had had with Breeze, searching every day for the babies' heartbeat and monitoring her contractions, hoping I would be a mother, or grandmother, once again. I had gone to bed with her for her premature labor in much the same way I had gone to bed myself while pregnant with Nathaniel, in a successful attempt to keep him safe inside until the proper time.

That kind of bond was strong enough to keep me from deserting my post, to make certain that I did a good job no matter how inconvenient, even if it was four in the morning. Strong enough for me to consider the puppies part of my own family once they slid out so helpless, blind, and able to do only one thing—suckle, just like a human baby. The only difference with puppies was that as a breeder, you were supposed to toughen your heart from day one, to remind yourself that you were going to be placing them; that expectation was supposed to be a buffer for the inevitable separation right from the beginning. Perhaps for some people it was easier to accept this.

Now, one more time, I looked over my file folder of puppy questionnaires from possible homes and leafed through the pile of those I had discarded. I had rooted out those who knew nothing about Dalmatians. I had crossed off the list a man who had three other dogs and whose first love was his bird sanctuary—nothing wrong with feathers, but my puppy was not going to come second to a bunch of birds. And then there was the woman who wanted to buy Green Bean for her husband's fortieth birthday, to ease his midlife crisis—I'd told her to bleach her hair and buy him a Porsche.

I thought over the homes for which they were about to leave, and I knew I had chosen well. But still, none of those places was here, in my capable and loving arms. I believe this is the regret, however fleeting for some, that every affectionate breeder feels as his or her puppies begin to make their way out into life.

All of them must leave me behind, and I would be hungry for that straight line of little faces peeking up over the walls of the puppy box in the morning, eyes bright and wide with the expectation of their food pan. I knew they were all going, each and every one, to people who were good and kind, to special places with special people to care for them. Or at least, I hoped, for you could never be certain, and sometimes a dog bounced back, sometimes a dog wound up in rescue, or worse, a kill shelter. Yes, despite my rationalizations, I would be bereft. For a while. And then I would heal. And then I knew I would do it all over again.

twenty-three

ONE BY ONE, THEY went. It was the right time, just before the first fear period set in, and thus the perfect opportunity for them to begin bonding with protective new owners, who would gradually replace their brothers and sisters and mother for emotional backup when a broom fell to the floor with a bang or a stranger approached.

When Purple left, the first break, we waved good-bye as Darcy, complete with her new name, and Christine drove off. Brad put his arms around me and gave me a hug.

Red was next, and as I put him into his mother's arms, I once again tried not to get emotional. He had been one of my special boys, the curious and confident one, the one that I probably would have kept if not for his patch. Barb and I had talked many times about this day, and she'd promised to take pictures right away and over the ensuing months so that I could watch him grow. She and her husband tucked "Riley" into their truck, and my arms felt emptier than ever.

I didn't understand why it was so hard to have this particular litter leave. Perhaps part of it was the impending loss of Myrna. I still visited her, spent afternoons with her in the

hospital when she was admitted for a variety of increasing difficulties, began to drive her once again to doctor's appointments—but it was obvious to me and most of our mutual
friends that there was less and less time left to her. Sometime
that month she took to bed after a surgery, and she never really
regained her feet. I began to mourn.

. . .

I distracted myself with the departure of the puppies, just as
I had tried to distract Myrna with their advent. After each
one left, Brad kept a countdown, saying, "and then there were
five," "and then there were four," "and then there were three,"
"and then there were two." Every time he did it, I gave him a
dirty look.

Blue was next, and this time I succeeded in restraining
myself, maybe because I was more prepared and less attached,
or maybe because the double-blue-eyed "Izzy" (a close name
to the one she had originally had in the puppy pen) was just
not one of the pups I'd grown really close to. Dawn waited a
few days before prying Pink out of my arms, but I knew that
I would see Adele many times, which I did, as she went on to
sweep up into the high rankings of the Dal statistics. Letting
them go didn't seem so hard anymore, and I grew a little more
confident that I was over the pain of this separation I had so
dreaded.

And that was when the home for Yellow fell through. Suddenly, instead of Green Bean being the only one unsold, there
were two. His new owners abruptly decided that they just didn't
want Yellow, though they had had more than two months to
think about it. I was angry at their unexpected about-face because we had turned aside others who had liked him best out

of the litter. One family, whose son had grown attached to him after several visits to the litter, had to be convinced to take a girl because the yellow pup had been spoken for.

Nevertheless, I tried to accept their decision with some equanimity: I reassured them that we didn't want them to take the puppy if they were at all uncertain. And this was true. The last thing I wanted was a puppy back with me when he was five months old, possibly untrained, perhaps unloved. As the cutest, most outgoing pup in the litter, Yellow would now be one of the last to go. He had been the under-ear patch in the group, and as such, his patch was nearly hidden, looking just like a very black ear. With a completely black one on the other side, he had a certain handsome symmetry to his face. He was growing more and more rambunctious with every day that went by, and I thought to myself that he was going to be a handful for whomever finally took him.

It didn't help that we hadn't placed Green Bean, either. He was getting increasingly dependent on me as the days went by, and it was hard not to favor him over Yellow, or to worry about him more, because Green Bean seemed to need me more. I knew I shouldn't care on such an intense level, but the fact was that I did. My relationship with Gulliver had been so different, as he had been the one who mothered me. When Green Bean snuggled in my arms and tucked his chin around behind my neck, I had to remind myself that I didn't want a shy, introverted dog who would need to be coaxed along. Nor did I want a dog who couldn't be shown in the breed ring.

And then suddenly Chrissy and Mike appeared, having seen the advertisement I'd run in the AKC breeder's section. They had just lost their beloved Dal to old age the month before. I was concerned that they hadn't done an appropriate amount of mourning to take on a new pup, but a friend reminded me that people grieve at their own rates. So I invited them over, feeling doubtful but willing to give the situation a shot.

They came to the house and tried to play with Green Bean, but he hid behind the couch. Mike put his head on the ground and shook his curls at him. Green Bean hid behind me. Chrissy tried to give him a cookie. Green Bean hid behind Brad.

They didn't seem to mind and said they wanted him anyway. I didn't like the situation, though. I wanted him to go off with tail flying, unafraid of the world. And so, over Dawn's objections, Brad and I kept him an extra week and hired a trainer to take him out on expeditions without me, so that he could experience a bit of the world without the buffer of his human mama.

As the end of week nine rolled around, I knew I had to let go. Although the week had helped his shyness, nothing was going to permanently solve it until he got into his new home and relaxed. And I worried that the fear period had begun; even more than before, he needed to bond with his new family rather than with us. So I told Chrissy and Mike to come and pick him up.

Fortunately, Green Bean was blissfully asleep on his bed when they arrived and didn't struggle or protest as I put him into Mike's arms. It was all so different from what I had imagined: the panicky struggle, the cries as he was packed into the car. Chrissy gave me a hug and promised the requisite pictures. We chatted for a while, as I made a great effort to maintain my composure and then wished they would just leave already. When the door closed behind them, I wept.

But Chrissy proved true to her word. She sent pictures almost immediately, and then, three times, a "letter from camp," written in Green Bean's voice, arrived on my email. Over the next few weeks, it became apparent that he was happy. They even decided not to rename him, and so he remained Green Bean. He had lost his shyness, it appeared, as he frolicked with friends and family across Chrissy's Facebook page. I liked to think that this was in part due to the extra time and attention I had given him, putting him on the road to his start in life.

But then there was Yellow. His small brown eyes were full of worry. He was stranded, right where he had grown up. At ten weeks, I wondered, *Where is he meant to be?*

· · ·

Even as I dreaded my last puppy leaving, still I was not happy about Yellow staying. Brad and I were growing attached to him as the days went by, but the calls for a male puppy did not come in.

We had hit a dry spell. Everyone who phoned wanted a girl, or a puppy for a lot less money, or they lived far away and didn't want to pay the extra to ship a puppy. And I didn't know how I felt about sending a puppy in the cargo hold of a plane anyway. I imagined his reaction: deep in the dark belly of the jet, frightened by the roar of the engines, desperate for a friendly face with no one to give it, needing to potty but nowhere to go. It just didn't seem right to me.

Finally, I got a call from a man who didn't seem to care what the dog looked like or who he was and simply wanted to arrange for "transport movers" to come and pick him up. In rapid-fire emails, he suggested that I give the moving company a check for taking the puppy, and then he would send on the rest of the fee. I said I needed to meet him first. He had to fill out an application. Did he have a fenced backyard? Who would take care of J.W. during the day while he was at work? As I got no answer to my questions, I began telling him that I wasn't interested in selling him a puppy. Nevertheless, he persisted. He was willing, he said, to pay more than I was asking for J.W., to compensate me for my extra time in coordinating with the movers. Understanding at last that I was being scammed, I emailed him angrily that I didn't place puppies via Allied Van Lines.

The weeks unfolded slowly. Twelve, thirteen, now fourteen, fifteen. Myrna was fading, and I was getting more and more attached to the one pup left here. He was so full of life.

Everyone else had gone home a month and a half ago. One Saturday at the end of September, Dawn and her husband and Brad and I went to a baseball game: the San Francisco Giants finally broke their losing streak, led by Cody Ross, who knocked several out of the park. Dawn turned to me. "That's it, Linda," she said with a smile. "Name the yellow puppy Cody." And so we did.

And in this way, at sixteen weeks, twice the length of time the other puppies had stayed with us, Yellow suddenly moved, late, beyond his puppy name into something more adult, even though we knew his eventual owners would undoubtedly change it. Day by day, we called him, "Cody, come!" and he did, responding more and more quickly to his new moniker, running from room to room with his black ears flying and his big puppy paws pounding the wooden floors.

He watched television every night with Brad and liked to follow the action on the screen with his ears perked up, whether it was a barking dog, a program on skunks, a loud truck, or Bette Davis. Nightly, we joked that instead of having "the head" (that delightful move Gulliver made when he put the warm weight of his head in your lap), we had "the hot bod," as Cody liked to deposit himself full-length across your legs.

After a while, I got jealous of his time with Brad and took the puppy, against my better judgment, with me into the bedroom, where I either watched television or read on the bed, leaning up against my pillows. I used to call Myrna around nine o'clock most nights, but now she was too weak to really talk, and so I spent most of the time with Cody.

He did one of two things as he lay on the bed with me: he either flung himself across my face (making it impossible for me to see anything with his hot little body in that position, and bending my glasses so I had to gingerly twist them back into shape), or he stretched himself across the bed full-length, on the other side, which made it impossible to cuddle and pet him. I would try to pull him back over next to me, and he would move right back to Brad's side of the bed. The first time he did it, I sighed at the futility of trying to relocate him and then smiled: maybe he just wasn't a bed cuddler like Gulliver. Another reason he should go.

And yet there was a look in his eye that reminded me of my special dog. Still, I wasn't so desperate, I thought to myself, desperate the way I'd been back in those dark years after Jim had left me and the only one I had to depend on was Gulliver. Maybe I didn't *need* another Gulliver. I certainly didn't *need* a patched dog.

None of this cute stuff mattered. Beneath my outward optimism when anyone asked about him going to a new home ("It's just a matter of time," I'd say with a casual shrug), I was worrying more and more: the older a puppy got, the harder it became to place him. People either wanted cute little bundles of fur at eight weeks, babies with whom they believed they could bond right away, or they wanted older dogs who were already trained: sit, down, off, stay, come—and perhaps the most important of all, potty! With his rapidly lengthening legs and more pronounced muzzle, when he stood up in his seat belt in the backseat of the car, he could nearly get his entire face out the window. Every day, Cody was beginning to look more and more like a dog and less and less like a puppy.

a different sort of dog

{IN ORDER OF APPEARANCE}

Cody

twenty-four

THE LEAVES ON THE few trees that did change color in the Bay Area began to turn in late October, just as Cody kept changing, too. Sailing season was still in its height, as on the West Coast, some of the best weather is in the autumn. On the boat, Cody turned out to be a natural sailor. Unlike Gulliver, he neither barked at the Jet Skis nor snarled or tried to attack other dogs when we went for walks. He attended his puppy kindergarten and played happily with other dogs even though he didn't pay too much attention to my commands to "sit" and "stay." The only trick he knew was "kissy face," which wasn't really a trick at all—just something he loved and didn't need to be told to do. Potty training was turning out to be a big job, and as I mopped up accident after accident, week after week, I groused about his possible lack of intelligence—as well as the chore of housebreaking someone else's dog.

At night, he went meekly into his crate and looked out from behind the grate with a pleasing expression on his face, while Breeze settled into her spot on her chair, and Brad and I got ready for bed and turned out the light. Unlike his mother— who as a pup had clawed at the door of the crate week after week when we put her in to sleep—Cody made it easy for us. With a sigh, he circled, plopped himself down, and made not another sound until morning, when he woke earlier than we did. Then I would roll over and hear him chewing patiently on his bone until we were willing to rise and open the bedroom curtains to the day.

He was a thoroughly calm and agreeable dog, except when playing with Breeze: he dominated her, climbing aboard her back and chewing on her neck, and she made no attempt to discipline him. We were stuck with yelling at him to get off, which he basically ignored. When he stole a dish towel or a roll of toilet paper, he paraded through the kitchen, proudly displaying his prize, and would come sheepishly to relinquish it if you called him sternly.

His big paws promised that he would be a big dog, and he liked to cock his head and look at you with his small round eyes, butt glued to the floor, as he waited patiently for a dog cookie. He had six small spots, the size a pinkie fingertip would make, which were smudged across the very end of his snout. This made him look as if he had been happily digging in chimney soot. And dig he did, making big holes in the yard and the garden, showers of dirt flying out from between his back legs, as if he were looking for buried treasure. I didn't understand it: he had plenty of bones in the house. I wiped off his paws, filled in the holes, and sighed in despair.

I had resolved not to get attached to him back at week ten. I kept reminding myself that he was a patched puppy, and a dark one at that, whom I could not show in the conformation ring.

All in all, he wasn't what I wanted.

I was stubborn about not giving in, even though Brad sent me appealing looks whenever he had him tucked up under his arm, or when Cody washed our faces with his long sticky tongue. I anticipated the crying I would do as I put him into someone else's arms, but I hardened myself against my emotions.

No calls.

And then, wham! He suddenly understood potty training and in the space of a day began holding his pee until I could get him outside when, with his nose, he rang the jingle bells that I had hung over the knob of the back door. Nevertheless, I ran a new ad in the AKC Breeder Section and put him up on Dawn's blog site, with a prominent photo filling the first page.

And then, one night, Brad asked me to sit down beside him and Cody where they lay on the couch.

"I don't think I can do it," he said.

"Do what?

"Give him up."

I reached down to stroke his soft coat and wondered who would be his mother and father, who would pet him if he left. Who would put down his food bowl? Who would tuck him into his crate at night? I had no answer for myself, or Brad, or him. I was, against my will, growing closer to him. I couldn't help it. He cocked his head like a dog in a television ad every time you asked him a question. He was too endearing. Too cute. Too willing. Too altogether perfect in his most imperfect of ways.

If Gulliver had been a "giver" and Green Bean more of a "taker," maybe Cody was the balance between the two. Secure, self-assured, able to love without losing himself.

And didn't I have to consider Brad's feelings? Wasn't he part of the decision as well? Another breeder told me that her kids always fell in love with at least one puppy in a litter and begged to keep him. "I just tell them no," she said, "and they get over it remarkably fast." Stung, I replied, "My husband isn't a child."

She stared back at me, clearly baffled.

I discussed the problem of Cody over and over with my psychiatrist. What should I do about this growing attachment? How should I handle it, extinguish it, learn to live with it— even though I knew I couldn't, and wouldn't, act on it?

"Sometimes," she said philosophically, "God gives you the dog you are meant to have."

That wasn't what I wanted to hear. But because it was Barbara who was saying it, I had to listen—despite my resistance.

Reluctantly, I began to write emails to breeder acquaintances who worked in obedience, asking if they had ever kept a dog from a litter who could not go on to work toward a conformation championship. Had they ever kept a dog purely to train in performance? But I also wondered, couldn't we have a third dog who was a pup from Breeze's next litter, who *could* be shown in both?

• • •

I was beginning, just beginning, to rationalize. If I couldn't show him in the conformation ring, maybe I could just train him to be a superb obedience dog, one of the caliber Rhiannon had been. I received answers back from those breeders to whom I had written that said no, they had never done that, but some said that they would, if they were in the same situation. One, a veteran in obedience whose scores were always in the high 90s, welcomed me "to the dark side." I laughed at that and felt a little more comfortable with the notion. A little, but still I wasn't convinced. I could not know then that Cody would turn out to be a High in Trial winner.

Simultaneously, I sensed those friends who were breeders in conformation shaking their heads. "He's not your Gulliver," one of them said to me. "How will you feel when Breeze has another litter and there is the perfect show boy?" asked another. And the most pragmatic of them all: "How would you fit three full-grown dogs on the boat?"

I had wanted to believe I wouldn't be influenced by others' opinions, but obviously, I was. I considered their points and wondered what kind of a breeder I was if I couldn't control my emotions enough to give away pups who were clearly unsuitable. You couldn't keep every one. And I thought also of Michele's old cliché: *if you can't stand the heat, get out of the kitchen.* But I remembered, too, Rhiannon—who hadn't been meant to stay, but who was the very first special dog to come into my life.

I went to the DCNC Specialty on Halloween weekend, and it hit me once again. On a beautiful sunny day, I watched the show dogs gait beautifully around the ring, free stack, and show themselves off to the judge. I was envious of Dawn, taking Breeze in and winning an Award of Merit. I did participate in the Parade of Winners and discovered that I was enjoying myself. I went home determined once again to place Cody with someone else. He could never stay with us because I wondered whether I would ever love him as much as I had Gulliver.

But once I got back and saw him nestled on the couch in Brad's arms, I wavered. As I wrestled with the problem once more, another idea came to me. I had always wanted to do therapy work with one of my dogs, to visit convalescent and elderly homes, hospitals for children and adults. Unfortunately, once the idea had occurred to me several years ago, I'd never owned the right dog. Rhiannon would have been perfect, but she was long gone. Breeze was too bouncy and was nervous around kids. Gulliver hadn't gotten along with other dogs, and usually you went with a team of handlers and dogs to the different sites. But Cody—why, Cody might just be perfect.

And it might be a way of expanding my life, of meeting new people and making new friends, of starting a new interest, one that was perhaps more fulfilling than showing. It could take me back to the charity work I had done for my temple with the soup kitchen and the Meals On Wheels program I had run, to the afternoons I had spent volunteering in my kids' schools. It would take me back to a far better place in my life, if only in this way. I signed up to be our club's liaison to the Dalmatian Club of America and contacted our rescue organization about writing better biographies for the abandoned dogs currently listed on the placement lists. I began to donate funds regularly to different Dalmatian shelters. I was trying to get out of my own little world.

And then there was "Furry Friends," a local organization that directed therapy dogs into different venues. I heard about it from a writer I didn't really know but with whom I had started emailing when she wrote to tell me how much she had liked one of my books. Maud Carol Markson had a rescued greyhound named Liberty, and before I knew it, I had a new friend and a writing compatriot who was a true dog person. I read her books and loved both of them. Calling "Furry Friends" myself, I discovered the specifics of the requirements for a therapy dog, learning what traits and how much training was required, and how old a dog had to be. I wanted to know what Cody and I could expect.

On the other hand, maybe he wouldn't make a great therapy dog. I had already accepted that he'd never show in the conformation ring. He was a different sort of dog, and suddenly, for no clear single reason, I was able to live with it. He would be my companion, and that was enough. It appeared that he did belong with us, in our home.

In just this way, with this one small step forward, I pushed away the doubts and decided.

What I knew, and that which was most important, was that he was becoming my heart dog. He was capturing me from head to toe, as surely as Gulliver had, though in a different way. I would continue to mourn that particular special dog, but my sorrow was eased. Now I could pass by his urn in the garden and ask him a question, or tell him that I was thinking of him, without disintegrating into tears. It wasn't time to take down the photos from the cabinet in my office, but that time was near.

And so Cody stayed, and he proved to be a unique dog. He lay at my feet while I worked, finding a patch of sun in which he could bathe. He waited patiently for his dinner, not dancing in agitated circles the way Breeze did, and often didn't even finish what he had been given unless I spiked it with some yogurt or canned meat. With the decision to have him stay came the inevitable and rapidly growing list of necessary nicknames: Code, CodyCodyCody, CodyCo, Codarino, Cody Man Cody Man, Snoops, Codalicious, Codariferae, Codarificarmente.

He turned out be a mischievous troublemaker unlike any other dog I had ever known. At first it was the morning glory vine that ran along the fence. It looked as luscious to him as a patch of corn to a crow, and while my back was turned, as I swept up the leaves that had just begun to fall, he nibbled away at it, right down to the stem; after half an hour, he came back into the house looking mysteriously sated and then began to throw up: once, twice, three times. Dogs throw up a lot, as I knew from the years of Gulliver's grazing, so I didn't worry at first, but when he expelled a violent rush of diarrhea that held nothing but bright red blood, I shoved him into the backseat of the car, forgot about the seat belt, and held my breath as I sped at eighty miles an hour to the animal hospital, sure he was bleeding internally. Then they told me that though morning glory was toxic, a dog would have to eat pounds of it for it to do any damage.

A few weeks went by, when, on a Sunday afternoon just before dusk, a huge patch of hidden mushrooms just around the back of my writing cottage caught his culinary attention. He didn't stop eating until he had to vomit. Once again, we were back on the highway doing eighty and hoping a cop wouldn't catch us. This time it was more serious. They detoxed him with activated charcoal but warned me that there would be a two-day wait till the blood panels came back and told us whether he was in danger of total liver failure. Over Monday and Tuesday we waited, watching to see if his eyes turned yellow, or if his usual happy gallop through the halls of the house deteriorated to a stagger, with the inevitable, painful death that would follow. Once again, he escaped damage.

But then, a week later, he did it another time. More detox, more astonishing bills from the vet, more frightened waiting for the call that might come bearing the news of his liver breaking down. Quickly, I became a mushroom forager, digging with my trowel desperately, staring at the ground until I saw double as I hunted down the brown and orange caps nestled under the pine trees on our property. The first day out, I collected a lawn-size trash bag filled with pounds of fungi and thought that if they had been chanterelles, I could have had a dinner party for thirty.

I cursed both his nose and his taste buds and his little, little brain. I couldn't remember any other dog I had ever owned being such a problem—not Penny, with her Happy Meal of Dad's zebra rug, not Daisy, with her penchant for chasing cars, and her early-morning squirrel trophies. Not even Gulliver, with his ingenious way of opening the trash can.

Two weeks later, I came out of the shower and heard him crunching away on some unlucky object. Still wet, quickly reaching for a towel, I searched, blindly, on the vanity counter for my glasses, so that I would be able to see. That was when it occurred to me exactly on what he was so happily munching away. When I finally recovered them they were scratched and bent beyond repair.

Next were my new hearing aids, left on a high counter he shouldn't have been able to reach. He chewed them into tiny, unrecognizable bits of metal, and as I searched for the rest, hoping at least one might be left untouched, I mourned the $7,000 this new set of aids had cost me only a month before he was born. They were insured—but still I had to fork over the $700 deductible. As I scoured the carpet for a missing transmitter and wire, I worried that whatever I couldn't find was nestled somewhere deep down in his gut, sharp enough to tear a hole. Scrupulously, I examined his poop for a week before I gave up on finding any of it.

Hearing aids were not the only things he liked to chew. Late one night, I woke from deep sleep to hear him throwing up again. I rushed to his side, knowing I had to examine the vomit to make certain there were no mushrooms in it. The vomit itself was bound together in a curious oblong shape, and as I tried to keep him from slurping it back down again, I realized there was no help for it: I couldn't reach the Kleenex before he gobbled it up, and I was going to have to pick it up with my hand. Holding it gingerly in my palm, I put it in the bathroom sink so that I could examine it. It was spongy and bounced back to the touch. No mushrooms were in evidence, and I breathed a sigh of relief. But then as I tugged on it, I slowly discovered that it could be unraveled. It was then I realized that he had chowed down on one of my nylon stockings. It had compacted into a mass that could easily have blocked his intestines.

And then there was my nighttime mouth guard.

It wasn't much longer before he cut his paw, deeply, all the way down through the pad, on a buried piece of chicken wire, while digging a hole to China in my garden. The wire was meant to discourage gophers, but it hadn't discouraged him. For three weeks, he hopped around on three legs, with the injured paw heavily bandaged and covered in a waterproof Muttluk. The bandage had to be changed every day, and we went through rolls of gauze and vet wrap. But he would lie quietly on Brad's lap in the evening after I had removed the bandage and rewrapped the foot, comically cooperating by extending his leg straight up into the air, which we quickly nicknamed "legus erectus."

All these antics, so unexpected and so undesirable, were part of this dog, and might continue to be so for quite some time, or possibly, forever. If he lived to be thirteen, I might be hunting mushrooms until I was seventy-one. Yet, perhaps not so surprisingly, he had already learned to cuddle with me on the bed—some of the time—with his soft warm muzzle tucked up tight under my arm. Or lying on his back with his hind legs opened trustingly to the world, so that his pink-and-black tummy was totally exposed, his paws curled on his chest, and his head cranked to the side like a contortionist. Breeze slept like a normal dog, curled tightly into herself, with the tip of her nose tucked up against the tip of her tail.

But as Brad and I looked back with pleasure at photos of the litter from the week when the pups turned three weeks old, we realized that this exposed position was exactly the one in which he had slept in the whelping box. Just as his brother, Riley, did so many miles away in Oregon. And just as Green Bean did in the Santa Cruz Mountains. It seemed odd that they all should manage such a strange position, and I wondered if it could have come down through the generations, just as Breeze's head butt had come from Jack. Had the pups inherited it from their father? When I checked with Linda and Doug Taylor, I was told that this was Mikey's preferred sleeping pose as well.

One night in late November, as I lay with him on my bed, reading, I paused for a moment. I was fondling his velvety soft ear. I realized that it was the black circular patch that I was gently rolling back and forth between my fingers. Somehow the sight of it didn't bother me anymore—either aesthetically, or for what it meant in terms of resuming a part of my life that had once given me such pleasure. It was a casual sort of thought, one I had come to indolently, and yet, simultaneously, it was also a revelation. The patch, the very thing that had so troubled me the first time I saw it when he was fresh and wet from his mother's womb, had become invisible to me. Now all I saw was Cody, his freckled face surrounded by two very black ears.

Somehow here I was, curled up seven months later with a dog I had very nearly let go. A new dog with his face on my pillow. A new dog to console me about the impending loss of Myrna. A new dog to fill my arms. Still, he was not Gulliver and never would be. He was not a show dog and never would be.

Nevertheless, I had overcome both my snobbery and my disappointment and gone on to love him just the same. He had turned out to be mine, despite all the hurdles, despite all the troubles. My heart held the affection for Cody that he so wanted, and his heart held the devotion that I had so hoped to have. I lay back and flipped to the page I had been reading with amusement. And so it was that one more time, a Dalmatian taught me exactly what I needed to know.

acknowledgments

My deep gratitude goes out to those who supported me as I wrote *Bespotted*:

First and last, my editor Dan Smetanka, who worked on *Bespotted* with a magic touch and whose faith in my writing enabled me to tackle a new subject—happiness.

Gail Hochman, my agent, who never gave up even with "a different sort of book."

Brad Clink, my husband, who lovingly perseveres despite it all and never (well, almost never) complains.

Joy Sexton, who bravely helped me remember much of our Dalmatian childhood—both the joy and the sadness.

Dawn Mauel and Michele Wrath, dear friends who generously gave "Dalmatian advice."

Carol Markson, a new compatriot who did a "first read" and offered great feedback.

John Freund, who gave his usual skilled critique.

Julie Kaufman, who has read with steadfast determination every one of my books over the course of more than twenty-five years.

Megan Fishmann, Kelly Winton, and Emma Cofod, my expert Counterpoint team, who shepherded the book through all its phases.

Rolph Blythe, Jack Shoemaker, and Charlie Winton, for publishing all three of my memoirs.